MY GIRL VAIDA

AN ADVENTUROUS HIKER, HER BIG YELLOW DOG, AND THEIR EVERLASTING BOND

CAITLIN QUINN

To all those who have lost someone who meant the world to them.

NewHampshire 4000 Footers White Mountains

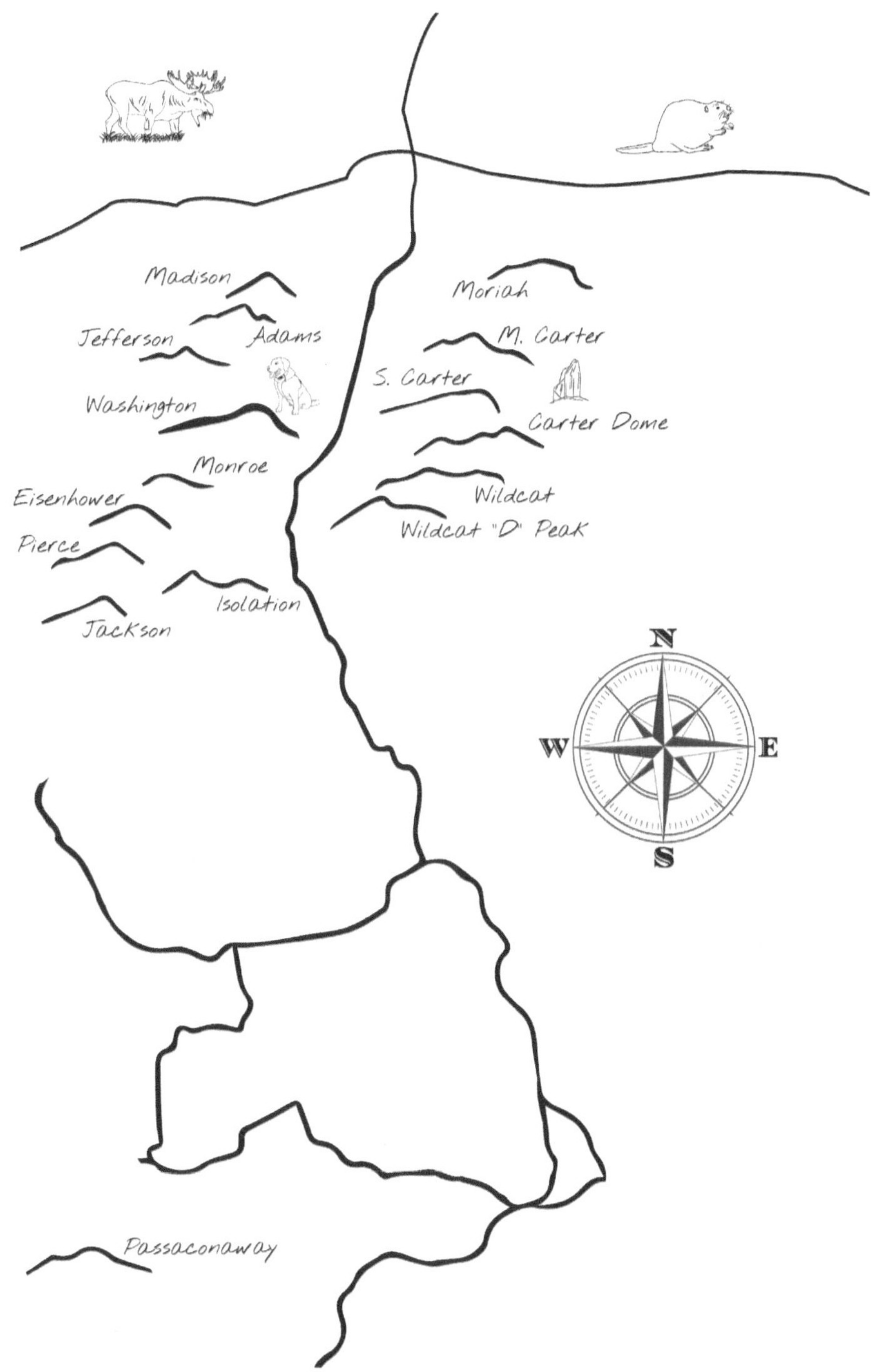

Madison
Jefferson
Adams
Moriah
M. Carter
S. Carter
Washington
Carter Dome
Monroe
Eisenhower
Wildcat
Pierce
Wildcat "D" Peak
Isolation
Jackson
N
W
E
S
Passaconaway

Table of Contents

PREFACE

I own nearly nothing, and I love to carry everything I need on my back in a tiny little backpack, but I carry a huge story to tell in my heart—a story that's still in the making.

I'm a lover, an adventurer, a make-no-plans-er, a see-what-happens-er. I'm a thirty-eight-year-old kid who likes to adventure out of a thirty-liter backpack and sleep in the dirt. I've chosen to live life differently. I don't care about the haves and have-nots. I seek the what-ifs.

I am not a writer. I am a thinker and a believer. People love the stories I tell, but that's just what I do. I tell stories and create memories, laughter, and "What the hecks?!" I can capture these moments through spoken word, and I know I can draw people in when I tell them, but I wasn't sure if I could write them. I wasn't sure if I could draw people in with written words the way I can with face-to-face storytelling. Despite this, I set out to document the legacy of Vaida—the world's best yellow dog and most loyal companion—in written form as a way for me to look back when I'm eighty-years old and smile and say to myself, *What a life we led!* But also, *What was I thinking?!* It's a way for me to share our wild and adventurous life and hopefully inspire a few.

None of this would have been possible without twelve-and-a-half years of Vaida by my side. With Vaida, I was truly never alone. I was never scared, never bored, and was always supported by her unconditional love for me as I in turn gave the same love and support to her.

Vaida was my adventure partner, my best friend, my partner in crime. She was my soulmate. My other half. She was who I spent my entire day with no matter what I was doing. She was who I kissed every night and said, "I love you, sweet girl." And on the rare occasion I did leave her side, I told her, "I love you more than all of the stars in the sky. I'll think about you the entire time that I'm gone."

I never worried about what people thought about me, my crazy life, or my sometimes questionable decisions, because in the end, I had Vaida. Always by my side, she was impossible not to love. Maybe it was her giant yellow hundred-pound frame that, despite its size, radiated a peaceful, gentle care and compassion, or her bright yellow eyes that looked straight into your heart and stole it as she stretched out her big yellow paw to show you she was there. Her presence breathed a calm, a sigh of relief, not just to me but to everyone she encountered. Vaida was my everything, and sometimes I think *we* somehow meant everything to a lot of other people. Vaida touched lives, and she helped me do the same.

During the writing process, when I was feeling a little stressed about the whole project, my mom asked me, "What do you do when you are faced with a challenge or difficult climb when you're hiking?"

I looked at her and said, "I deal with it. I buckle down and get through it. I look at it as something I know I can overcome."

I am stubborn, riddled with strength, grit, and determination. So I powered through the book, and now you're holding our story in your hands. The details of our story are as I remember them, told from my perspective, and may not exactly align with the memories of others. The conversations I recall are not verbatim but are my best recollection of what was said in that particular moment. While the precise words may now escape me, the memories of the twelve-and-a-half years Vaida and I spent together, attached at the hip, never fade.

Vaida truly lived a beautiful, arguably unrivaled life, and I wanted to see that story come alive on paper. I hope that when you read this book, you can understand what a remarkable dog she was, what an amazing journey we had together, and will be inspired to find your own source of life-altering transformation. And I hope that if you have ever lost anyone who meant the world to you, you will be able to find healing within.

—Caitlin (and Vaida)

1

Arkansas's Amber Becomes Vermont's Vaida

I was in kindergarten when my parents got our first dog, a purebred golden retriever. I remember having Casey for quite a few years and being very close to her. We got our second dog three years later, when my parents bred Casey. I was in third grade when she had the litter and remember my brother and I being really excited about it, not only because we got to name the puppies but because we were going to keep one and have a mother and son. The one we kept was a male we named Big Blue because he was the biggest boy and wore a blue yarn around his neck during his first nine weeks in the whelping box. We eventually changed his name to just Blue and, of course, bought him a blue collar.

It seemed like there were always golden retrievers at my house, especially when I was a young child. Dogs have been part of my life for as long as I can remember, though I don't know why my parents chose to get our first dog, or why it was a purebred golden retriever. It could have had something to do with the fact that my brother and I, like a lot of young kids, simply wanted a dog. My mom had grown up with dogs, and she probably just wanted us to experience life with one too.

What I remember most about having dogs as a kid was their companionship and their loyalty. Casey was my first dog and always my favorite. She wasn't as good-looking or playful as her son Blue, but she was a very sweet girl. Plus, she had this great trick where she could fit three tennis balls into her mouth at once. She was always there for me, this incredibly mellow friend who could always make me smile. I learned the importance of having a dog around that you could count on to be your friend, a friend who was always there when you got home.

My brother was a year-and-a-half older and a grade ahead of me in school, and we were never really that close. In fact, we were only really close when he had me pinned down and was rapidly tapping on my chest just to annoy me. Growing up, I always felt like I was living in his shadow. I was a tomboy, and I was very shy. Sure, I had friends, but he seemed to have way more. And at the time, he was the one excelling at sports while I was still struggling to find confidence in my athletic skills. But when I would lie on the floor with Casey or play fetch with her in the yard, she was the only teammate I needed and the feelings of being a loner faded away.

I grew up in western Massachusetts and went to the University of Vermont on a softball scholarship, thanks to my athletic skills developing over time. While I was away at college, I can't say I missed having a dog. I was so motivated by sports that there wasn't time to think about my dogs back home. Wrapped up in the excitement of being a young adult and finding my way in the world, my close relationship with dogs seemed to be an elementary school thing that had passed.

I stayed in Burlington, Vermont after graduation and got a job as the office manager at a live-music concert venue called Higher Ground. Thoughts of getting a dog were still a few years away.

In spite of living in one of the most beautiful states in New England, I was not into the outdoors and hiking yet. Then, a couple of years after I graduated, I dated a guy named Mike who took me on my first hike up a nearby mountain called Camel's Hump, one of the taller peaks in Vermont. You could see its distinctive profile from the softball field I played on every single day at UVM. But if someone had pointed to it and said, "What's that?" I would have said, "I don't know. It looks like any old mountain to me." As it turned out, Camel's Hump wasn't any old mountain—it was the mountain that completely changed my life. Dating Mike didn't go anywhere, ended after only a few months, but I'll always remember him fondly for having introduced me to hiking.

On that first hike up Camel's Hump, I had no idea what to do or what to wear or what to bring. I'm pretty sure I wore cotton corduroy pants, which I have subsequently learned is definitely not appropriate hiking gear. Experienced hikers will tell you "cotton kills" because cotton retains moisture from your sweat, snow, or rain, and this could lead to hypothermia. Thankfully I didn't have to deal with any of those things on my first hike and have since learned about more appropriate hiking attire.

I had always been team-sports oriented. Through elementary and high school and then four years of Division I softball, working hard with teammates and having a coach to direct and guide me was all I had known. I was used to running fast to first base or diving for a line drive. Things that were over in an instant. I didn't know what it was like to walk for miles and work really hard for two hours to get to the top of a mountain and then be rewarded with an incredible view. Hiking was so different—I'd never done anything like that before. It was something I could do on my own, whenever I felt like, with no team members or companions required, no one to tell me how slow or fast to go or which trail to take. I was absolutely in awe.

When I find something I like, I stick to it. I admit, I wasn't the greatest athlete, but I had the dedication and drive to take my average athletic skills and make them above average. So, the day after that first hike up Camel's Hump, I went out and bought a book called *Hiker's Guide to the Mountains of Vermont: 100 Best Hikes in Vermont*, and hiking became an obsession.

The feelings I had experienced playing highly competitive softball were pretty amazing. Hiking gave me the same feelings. The rush and the high that I used to get at the end of a winning playoff game, when someone drove in the winning run or made an amazing play to win a game, was exactly how I started to feel when I got to the top of the mountain. But the difference was that those feelings were based on a moment, over in an instant. With hiking, it took hours to reach the top of the mountain. That's when the familiar rush hit me, after extended periods of hard work and focus. I was probably thinking, *Holy shit, this is really hard*. But once I got to the top I thought, *Holy shit, this makes all of this really worth it*. Instead of a trophy or the pats on the back from teammates, it was the mountain air and beautiful views that provided me with enjoyment and a sense of accomplishment.

When I first caught the hiking bug, I was working nights and didn't have to go in until five or six in the evening, so I often set out on an adventure before work. I got used to hiking alone because I had the whole day available and all of my friends were at their day jobs. I also didn't care if anyone else could come with me, which may not have been smart, in retrospect. Because I was so new to hiking, I didn't know anything about the potential dangers of hiking alone, like getting lost or getting caught out in drastic weather changes. I would simply open up my new hiking guide, see something that was forty-five minutes or an hour's drive away, and head there. I'd get home in time to get ready for work, often excited to share with my coworkers what I had done that day. I was hiking alone probably 95 percent of the time and slowly becoming known for my adventurous endeavors. Fortunately, during my early hiking years, I never experienced any of the dangers of hiking alone.

My family and friends were excited I'd found this new passion. I'm sure my mom was a little nervous that I was always going off on my own, but I always made sure to tell her when and where I was going and what trail I was taking. If I remembered, I would call and let her know when I was safe. I didn't always remember. She never forgot to call and check when I didn't, though.

As time went on, I discovered that hiking without anyone else better suited my quiet, somewhat shy personality. I had also realized that, while I enjoyed hiking with friends from time to time, it was really nice not having to make plans with anyone. Plus, I was working late and never knew what time I'd wake up in the morning. What I did know was that every day I had a large chunk of time before work that I wanted to fill with hiking. And even though I worked in a highly social environment and met a lot of people, some with a similar passion, I still preferred being by myself because I could go where I wanted, anytime I wanted, and at my own pace. So I spent the next two or three years of my early twenties hiking on my own.

It was when I met my friend Leah that I started to think about getting a dog to join me on my adventures. Leah was standing outside of her store in Burlington with her two big, beautiful dogs one day when I walked by. I stopped in my tracks when I saw her dogs. Cookie looked like a huge red female lion with a wrinkly head, and Bella had this commanding presence with her two canine teeth poking out above her bottom lip. She was large and intimidating, but once you met her and looked into her soulful eyes, you found she was really sweet. I'll never forget how my dad would refer to her as "Sad Sack" because of the expression she had on her face. I had never seen dogs like that before. I didn't know this woman, but I had to talk to her. Leah told me that Cookie was a French mastiff and Bella was a bull mastiff, then added, "I recognize you from Higher Ground! I go to shows there all the time." Then I stood outside her store asking her a million questions about her dogs.

They were both beautiful, unique-looking dogs, though to me, Cookie was not only unique but absolutely stunning, jaw-dropping, and head-turningly beautiful. If you saw Leah out with her dogs in public, it would be impossible to not stop and ask about them. I used to like to walk around with Leah just so I could be seen with the dogs as well, having discovered I enjoyed the attention they generated. Maybe I wasn't so shy after all, or at least didn't want to be.

Leah and I continued to cross paths at Higher Ground, and our friendship evolved from there. We were drawn to each other back then and are still close friends today.

By this time, I had been hiking for a couple of years, was still working nights at Higher Ground, and had started dating a guy I met at work named Garett. He had a dog, a shepherd/husky mix named Jerry that was always with Garett no matter what he was doing or where he was going. Garett worked for a log home restoration company, so Jerry got to spend all day with him on the jobsite. In his free time, Garett liked to travel and go to concerts. Jerry would be his copilot and then hang out in the car while Garett was in the venue watching the show. I thought it was really unique that someone who was constantly out and about always had his loyal sidekick with him.

Sometimes I would take Jerry out for long walks, and between these excursions with Jerry and my time spent with Leah's two mastiffs, I started thinking about getting my own dog. Ultimately, it was seeing Garett and Jerry together, seeing that it was possible to always have your dog by your side, that made my decision a lot easier. That's what I wanted, that constant companionship.

Once I decided I wanted to get a dog, I honestly wanted a mastiff. I found a website called Petfinder.com, which allowed me to limit my search to French mastiff. Unfortunately, they were all far away, in states like Pennsylvania, Ohio, and Texas. I realized that part of why I wanted a dog was for my hiking adventures, which was how I spent most of my free time by that point. Because all of the French mastiffs were so far away and I didn't know how good they would be hiking long distances or with getting a lot of exercise, I gave up on the mastiff idea and started looking at dogs that were available closer to where I was in the Burlington, Vermont, area. I was living by myself in this beautiful old farmhouse. It had a giant glass window looking out at a picturesque barnyard with horse pastures and a big, red barn, the perfect setting for a dog.

The dogs on Petfinder were listed with pictures and descriptions, and you could use the search feature to narrow down your results with a number of filters. After giving up on mastiffs, I used the search filter to look at dogs that were available within a hundred-mile radius. I knew I wanted a larger breed, and although I would have taken a young dog, I wasn't looking for a really young puppy. I guess it was kind of vain, but I wanted to know what the dog would look like when it got older. Puppies can change a lot as they grow. Essentially, I was looking for a large breed that was a little bit older. It didn't matter to me if it was male or female. The same day that I decided to stop looking for a mastiff and start looking at what was available closer to me was when I came across Vaida.

I'll never forget when I saw her adoption photo. It was a gorgeous sunny spring day. I was on my computer before work, searching for dogs on Petfinder, when a picture popped up of a bright yellow dog with stunning yellow eyes and soft liver-pink pigment. The dog was available through a local rescue organization, Golden Huggs Rescue in Vermont. The listing said the dog's name was Garrett, and I immediately fell in love with him. This was it. This was the dog I wanted. He had beautiful yellow eyes that seemed to look right into my heart and soul.

I got a kick out of the fact that the dog I wanted to adopt was named Garrett and my boyfriend's name was also Garett, just spelled differently. Garett was actually hanging out at my house that afternoon, so I got up from my computer and ran to the other room shouting, "Garett, you've got to see this dog. It's incredible. It's beautiful. Look at those eyes, and his name is Garrett. How funny is that?" The coincidence was too much to ignore. "I'm getting this dog," I said.

I emailed Golden Huggs Rescue and told them I came across Garrett's photo and his description on the adoption page and wanted to adopt him. They sent me an application, and I quickly filled everything out. When they got back in touch, they told me it looked like I was qualified, so they would just need to do a home visit and a couple of screening processes first before they could make a final decision.

But I was totally unprepared for what was said next. Garrett was way more than a hundred miles away—he was actually in Arkansas. I thought, *What the hell? You're a rescue out of Vermont. What do you mean he's in Arkansas?* After I politely asked why they were posting for adoptions so far away, they explained that Golden Huggs Rescue is made up of a very small group of volunteers who work with rescue partners outside of New England to find loving, suitable homes for displaced, abandoned, or stray dogs with golden personalities. The dogs they rescue have either been relinquished by their owners, found as strays, or abandoned at the shelter door. They went on to say that once a dog was ready for adoption and matched with a new owner, the dog would be transported. I thought that was a really cool concept but also kind of bizarre because I wanted to meet the dog first, to be sure we were a good match. I was told that dogs were not transported until there was a designated adopter, but they could put me in touch with the current foster mom so I could ask more questions.

I was able to connect with the foster mom in Arkansas and she told me Garrett, who she was fostering along with his brother and sister, was a great dog and he and his siblings got along well with all of the other foster dogs. Because the website only had one picture of him, I asked her to send me more photos. I was surprised and confused when her email arrived. Garrett did not look like the dog I had asked about. He was a beautiful yellow retriever-looking dog, but he wasn't the stunning, yellow-eyed dog I had seen in the photo on Petfinder. This dog had a black nose, black pigment, and dark brown eyes.

Confused, I emailed Golden Huggs and said, "You guys put me in touch with Garrett's foster mom. She told me more about him and sent me some photos, but it doesn't look like the dog I had asked about."

Golden Huggs wrote back, explaining that they had mixed up the photos and descriptions of the two yellow dogs on the Petfinder post. They'd accidentally posted the photo of the yellow female with the yellow eyes, whose name was Amber, with the description of her brother, Garrett, the yellow male with the dark eyes.

When they asked me if I wanted the male or female, I told them I didn't care as long as it was the one with the yellow eyes. They said that was Amber, Garrett's sister, and I told them that I wanted Amber, the girl with the yellow eyes.

A few days later, Golden Huggs sent a volunteer to my house to do a home visit, after which they told me I was adoption qualified. I was then able to talk to the foster mom again and asked about Amber specifically. I was pleased when she told me that Amber was not like the other dogs, was not bouncing off the walls or running around or really needing activity or attention. I remember telling her that sounded great because I really liked the idea of a mellow dog. I couldn't resist asking her if she thought Amber would go on hikes with me.

I don't know if she was able to give me an honest opinion, if she understood the demands of hiking, but I do remember her saying that she wasn't like the other dogs. I had a really good feeling about Amber. I began making the arrangements with Golden Huggs and expected to get Amber in about a week.

When I adopted Amber, I was told she was about six months old, weighed approximately fifty pounds, and one of her parents was a golden retriever and one was a Newfoundland. I was never quite sure that was the case. One of my friends used to jokingly refer to her as a "golden muttriever" because he thought she was just a mutt. A perfectly yellow-y golden-y mutt. I had the chance to meet her other brother because he was adopted in Vermont as well. He looked just like her but was chocolate brown, with the same stunning yellow eyes and liver pigment. That's what always made me think she was more Labrador retriever than golden retriever, so it made sense that I always told people she was a Labrador/ Newfoundland with probably a few more breeds mixed in.

I was still working at Higher Ground when I adopted Amber in June of 2009. There were probably around forty of us working together, and we were one big family; everyone knew and loved each other. We liked to joke around and make fun of each other. We all did it, and no one really minded because it was all done in the name of fun and games. So it was no big surprise that my coworkers were involved in Amber's forever name.

At this time, Higher Ground was doing a series of outdoor concerts at a museum in Shelburne, Vermont. After one concert by David Byrne, the lead singer of Talking Heads, I was cleaning up and talking with my coworker Jess, when another coworker, Troy, joined us.

Jess said, "Caitlin is going to be getting a dog."

Troy said, "What are you going to name her?"

I said, "I don't know, Troy. I have no idea. I'll probably just wait until I meet her. Her name is Amber right now, but I think that is really lame. I'm definitely not keeping that."

Troy turned to me and said, "You should name your dog Vaden." Vaden was the last name of one of our coworkers.

I said, "Troy, that's the dumbest idea I've ever heard, to name my dog after Nick Vaden. That's ridiculous." Based on how we were always kidding around with each other and the stupid jokes we would make, I guess it would be a typical Higher Ground thing to suggest naming my dog after a coworker.

Even though I'd quickly dismissed Troy's suggestion, it did remind me of the girl in the early 1990s movie, *My Girl*, with Macauley Culkin, but I wasn't exactly sure of her name. Later, when I got to my phone, I looked up the movie. I was right. Her name was Vada, and that was perfect because this dog was going to be "my girl." I decided to spell the name differently, V-A-I-D-A, thinking this would make it easier to pronounce. The name fit. From the second I got her, she was definitely "my girl."

On June 6, 2009, a very beautiful, sweet six-month-old Vaida arrived on a transport truck from Arkansas, organized by Golden Huggs Rescue. Her eyes were just as stunning as in the photos that had captured my heart a few weeks prior. She was everything I was hoping for and more. I'll tell you more of the story about when I got her in the next chapter.

Vaida and I bonded very quickly. That was a good thing, because she was the first dog I ever had on my own and I had no idea what I was doing. We became best friends and began to trust one another almost immediately. It helped that, like me, she was so laid back. When I got her, I had this vision, which may have even been from my childhood, of an old man farmer in his pickup truck with his dog always next to him. That's what I wanted. As soon as I decided to get a dog, I wanted a dog who was going to go everywhere with me. I wanted a dog who was always going to be with me.

I finally had a hiking companion I didn't have to make plans with. All I had to do was pack my bag and say, "Come on, sweet girl," and Vaida was ready and willing to go. Almost every day before work, we would go on long walks or short local hikes. Two or three days a week, we got to go on bigger hikes. Other days, we would find a place where she could take a dip. She loved the water and loved to swim.

Any time you saw me, you saw Vaida, because we were always together. Whenever I had to go into town to run errands, Vaida came along, patiently waiting in the car or tied up outside the store until I returned. Because she was so well-behaved and I trusted her, if there was nothing for me to attach her leash to, I'd make her leash look like it was attached to something and do my errand. I knew she wasn't going anywhere. Most times when I came back out, she was flopped on the sidewalk with people petting her.

Of course, I often went places where she could accompany me inside. The bank stops were her favorite since she could come inside with me and get treats. Our main bonding was everyday life, being together no matter what I was doing. Vaida's gentle, calm demeanor made it possible to do all these things without even thinking about it.

Vaida seemed to enjoy our walks in downtown Burlington, near where I lived at the time. Burlington is the largest city in the state, and it has a great pedestrian marketplace on Church Street. Its large number of shops, restaurants, and cafés make it a popular place to visit for both locals and tourists. Vaida got to meet a lot of people on these walks, most of whom could not get over the sight of this big, beautiful yellow dog with a mellow personality and stunning yellow eyes ambling alongside me. Whenever they fawned over her, it reminded me of the first time I saw my friend Leah with her two dogs. Vaida was drawing attention just like Cookie had caught mine. As we began to meet more people and more and more strangers' hands patted her big yellow head, I started to notice I was slowly becoming a little less shy. A shell I had been carrying with me since I was a child living in my big brother's shadow was starting to break down.

Leah's store was adjacent to Church Street and happened to be right next door to my favorite restaurant in the world, Stone Soup. My favorite errand was to go visit Leah, leave Vaida with her in her store, and get some food from Stone Soup. It wasn't unusual for Leah to report that a number of people came into her store just because they saw Vaida through the window. One time I even returned to find Vaida sitting quietly in the store with a huge sign Leah had placed around her neck that said, "For Sale - One Million Dollars." Thankfully, no one bought her.

Dogs often can add a level of chaos to human situations. They need to be paid attention to, especially if they are playing, running around, sniffing, barking, or simply being dogs, but Vaida was the complete opposite. Whenever she entered a room, it always seemed like there was a change in energy. She brought a sense of calm into every situation. When

I would introduce her to friends or bring her to new places, the reaction was never "Oh my gosh, what are you doing with this dog here?" It was more like, "Oh, wow, I needed this today."

2

You Brought Your New Puppy to Work?!

When I first started college, I was really into live music. Little did I know when I headed to the University of Vermont on a softball scholarship in 2001 that there happened to be a live-music concert venue called Higher Ground within walking distance of the campus, in a small town called Winooski. I went to a couple of concerts a month at Higher Ground before I started working there three-and-a-half years later, most often with my teammate, Kelli. We were the rule-bending, somewhat devious girls on the softball team who somehow managed to do stuff that generally would be frowned upon by the coaching staff. That included going to Higher Ground as often as we could. Most shows were eighteen-plus and the drinking age was twenty-one. Anyone under twenty-one had their hands marked by security with a big black X using a permanent marker that wasn't easy to wash off. The coaches never liked seeing the black smudges on our hands at 6 a.m. practice because they knew we'd been out late the night before. In spite of that, I continued to attend concerts weekly. Sorry, coach.

During my freshman year, I landed an internship with a juice company called Nantucket Nectars, and one of the ways we promoted the product was by handing out free samples to concertgoers at Higher Ground.

As a result, I was able to get to know the staff, and this connection often allowed me and my UVM friends to cut the line when we went to shows.

By the time my senior year rolled around, I really wanted to work at Higher Ground but knew that getting my foot in the door wouldn't be easy. Higher Ground was hands down the coolest nightclub in Vermont, and most of the staff had been working there for many years. Then I came up with an idea—I was an anthropology major, so why not do an anthropological study of the night life? Maybe, if I could convince my professor of the idea, I could do an internship. Using my best powers of persuasion, I got her to agree. Now all I needed to do was convince someone at Higher Ground that it was a great idea.

I was able to get the contact info for one of the owners, Kevin, and I sent him at least five emails saying, "I want to do an internship with you for college credit. It won't cost you anything." I never received a response. Just as the deadline for submitting internship plans was approaching, I sent one more email with a new subject line, "Free work is around the corner." I guess this caught his attention because he decided to take me on as an intern.

At that point, the small club in Winooski had been closed for a few months due to a city redevelopment project, so my internship was working with Kevin to open a brand-new, larger venue in South Burlington Vermont, still very close to UVM. Kevin and I worked together in a small office adjacent to the demolished venue in a beautiful, old mill building overlooking the Winooski River. I was opening mail, answering the phone, and helping pick out paint colors for the green rooms as we converted an old five-screen movie theater into two concert spaces, one with a capacity of around 300 and the other with closer to 750. We were writing the business prospectus and searching for investors for the new club. I thought it was so cool that we were sending letters to folks like Ben and Jerry of the well-known Vermont ice cream company or members from Vermont's famous band Phish. I was Kevin's right-hand person. This allowed me to make good on the requirements of my internship. Interestingly, the most important thing I learned was not to call anyone who works in a night club before noon.

As the fall internship was ending, I said, "Kevin, thank you so much for the opportunity. This has been a great experience."

He said, "What? You're not going anywhere. The new club we've been working on is opening in the beginning of December. I still need your help."

He gave me twenty hours per week. That meant going into December and the soon-to-be spring semester of my senior year, I already had a job lined up. The twenty hours quickly turned into twenty-five, thirty, and eventually forty hours per week. We opened the club December 2, 2004 with a band called Hot Tuna.

Because of my new job, I knew I would not have time to dedicate to the sport I had loved and played since I was a kid. This was not an easy decision, but I was well aware of the fact that it was time to prepare for life after softball, and this awesome job I had worked so hard to get was going to afford me that opportunity. I decided to give up playing softball after the fall season even though I knew that meant giving up my athletic scholarship. I was so excited for this new, fun opportunity, but I was not so sure my parents would be. It wasn't exactly the vision they had for me after my four years of working very hard to obtain a degree in Arts and Sciences with an Anthropology major. At least I was working in the Arts field, though, right?

While on the one hand, thoughts of now working full-time at the coolest concert venue in the entire state of Vermont was exciting, on the other hand, I was very intimidated by thoughts of this highly social environment I would find myself in on a daily basis. Not only was there potential for the club to be bustling with upward of one thousand people on any given night, but also most of my coworkers had been working there for years and were very close-knit. I was the young, shy newbie who didn't quite feel like she fit in. When I first started working there, I usually bolted right at the end of my shift while all of my coworkers gathered at the bar.

At the new Higher Ground location in South Burlington, our of-fices were upstairs, looking down from the old movie-theater projection rooms. I had my own desk right around the corner from Kevin's, and my title was office manager. I was doing all of the accounting and en-tering all of the data into QuickBooks and was also responsible for the month-end reconciliations. I went to work at six in the evening. Usually the doors opened at seven or eight, so Kevin and I spent the first hour or two discussing accounting matters and setting up the cash registers. After that, I basically spent the concert evening making sure the bars had change, seeing some friends as time allowed, and watching the show for a little bit. In between, I would touch base with Kevin and we would do a few hours of office work. He is a laid-back, really nice guy who loves music. His brother-in-law is the lead singer for the very famous jam band from Vermont called Phish. When Kevin was in his early twenties, he lived on the New Jersey shore. It was there that he really got into the music scene and all that the 1970s had to offer. As a result he had a lot of crazy stories to share. That's how he developed a huge love of music. He was a really cool guy to work for. Sometimes he gave me a bartending shift instead, which I liked because I got to watch the concerts and was able to make a little more money that way. I probably would have made more in tips had I not always looked so serious. I used that face to mask how I really felt on the inside—shy and intimidated by my surroundings.

That was the setting for my life when I decided to get a dog. Pretty chaotic.

I had been working at Higher Ground for a little over four years on the day Vaida arrived on the truck from Arkansas. It was Saturday, June 6, 2009. Unfortunately, I had made plans months prior to go to a Phish concert with my boyfriend Garett in Mansfield, MA. Luckily, when I asked my parents to go get her for me, they agreed. I was disappointed about not being able to get her myself because it would have been really special to see her come off the truck and into my arms. That was a decision that to this day I regret. I should have been the first one to greet her.

The next morning, we drove to Amherst, Massachusetts to my parents' house to get Vaida. We then had a three-hour drive back to Vermont in order for me to get to work. Vaida was incredible from the start, sweet and mellow. Getting Vaida from my parents was a whirlwind. I don't remember much other than needing to get on the road and her sleeping the entire car ride back.

As we drove back to Vermont, it occurred to me, *Oh shit, I just picked up this huge new responsibility. I don't have any roommates to help me, so I need to figure out how I am going to work tonight and take care of this brand-new puppy. Actually, most nights for the foreseeable future for that matter. This is quite the responsibility I just took on.*

I had to bartend that night and was running late but had to swing by my house first to get ready. I brought Vaida inside and showed her where she would be living, then realized I simply couldn't leave her there alone on her very first day. I decided she was coming to work with me. When

I got to Higher Ground, I pulled up to the back door where all the buses parked and, with Vaida by my side, we walked in. When we walked in the door, the security guard looked at me, looked at my new puppy, and said, "What are you doing?!"

I explained to him that I had just gotten her, was running late, and couldn't leave her home alone. In a rush, I tried taking her up the cement stairs to the office, but it quickly became apparent she had never climbed stairs before. Now I needed the security guard's help. We walked past the artists' green room and opened the door to the office just as Kevin was coming around the corner. He looked at me, looked down at Vaida, and said, "You brought your new puppy to work?!"

I knew Kevin very well at that point and could tell he wasn't actually upset, just in shock, especially because I didn't give him any notice. I looked down at Vaida already sitting at my feet, not even curious about this wild environment, and then back up at Kevin and said, "I'm sorry, Kevin. Garett and I were at the Phish show last night, picked her up today, and I was running late. I didn't know what else to do."

Still in shock, he expressed his concern that she was going to be peeing and pooping all over the place. I told him that would not be the case even though I could not be sure, then crossed my fingers as I walked away.

I put a little blanket down next to my desk and put her on it. I told her to stay put and ran down to the bar to work. Every time a security guard or a sound guy walked by, I would ask, "How's Vaida? What's she doing?" Their response was always the same, "Caitlin, she hasn't moved." That night, a loud gypsy punk band called Gogol Bordello was playing and the walls were literally shaking. Vaida slept the entire night. She did not pee or poop in the office. In fact, I'm not even sure if anyone took her out to potty, but it definitely wasn't me. I was too busy working a sold-out show. It was quite the memorable first night with her.

At the time, I lived in a farmhouse on a dirt road that was a perfect setting for the bonding experience. Sometimes we would play in the yard or go for a walk on the many rarely traveled dirt roads in the area. I also frequently took Vaida to the busy pedestrian marketplace, Church Street, in Burlington. There were always tons of people strolling about, and I enjoyed walking around with Vaida and watching as they "oohed" and "aahed" over her. She really was quite the sight with her pretty yellow coat and stunning yellow eyes as she ambled alongside me on a loose leash, simply observing all of the people and all that was around her.

I also liked to take Vaida swimming a lot. She loved to swim in any body of water: lake, stream, river. But then, of course, I also loved to take her on hikes. When I first got her, I often took her up a local, small mountain called Mount Philo. Then, within the first two months of having her, I expanded our hikes to include Camel's Hump and Mount Mansfield, which are both over four thousand feet in elevation (Mount Mansfield is the highest peak in Vermont). She easily managed the physical demands of hiking and loved being outdoors. We hiked as often as we could, usually at least a couple times a week. I remember watching her puppy muscles grow as she went from fifty pounds to eighty pounds before I knew it.

On days when we couldn't hike, we stayed around the house and spent time in the large yard. Her favorite toy was her Jolly Ball, which was a red rubber ball the size of a soccer ball with a knotted rope running through the center. She loved playing with the Jolly Ball in the yard, chasing it when I threw it and shaking it when she got ahold of it. She also loved chasing sticks and would chase them until I grew tired of throwing them.

Because Vaida's first night at Higher Ground had been such a success and Kevin didn't seem to mind, I was comfortable bringing her to work a few times a week. I'm not sure I ever actually asked Kevin if he was okay with me bringing her—she just kind of became the unspoken mascot. Plus, I could just see how much joy she brought everyone, including Kevin. When she did come with me to work, she got to pretty much go everywhere I went and experience everything at Higher Ground. She got to go in the green rooms, listen to sound checks before the concerts, and sometimes even spend time on the concert floor. For the most part, however, Vaida spent the majority of the evening sleeping under my desk while I worked in the office. Whenever I had to leave the office, I had no problem leaving her there because I knew she wouldn't budge or bother anyone. I was proud of her.

Next to the office was a hallway that was restricted to management, artists, and their crew. Sometimes I would walk through the hallway with Vaida, and it was not unusual for the bandmembers to say, "Oh my gosh, a dog. I miss my dog at home. Can the dog come in here?" I was happy to let her go in the green rooms because she was so well-behaved.

She would go in and sit on the couch with the artists, and they would talk to her and pet her. Sometimes the bands were enjoying her company so much I would leave her with them and go back to work. It always made me feel good that other people liked having her around as much as I did, especially rock stars and famous people. Wandering the halls of Higher Ground over the course of four years, Vaida got to interact with acts such as The Black Crowes, Ray LaMontagne, and also members of Phish, Grateful Dead, and Wu-Tang Clan. Had Snoop Dogg ever played at Higher Ground, I wouldn't have been surprised if Vaida got to paw-bump him.

Vaida also got to listen to sound checks, which can be a pretty noisy experience, especially for a dog, but she never seemed to mind. Sound checks got pretty loud when there was no one in that large room to absorb the sounds coming from the huge speakers. She was never startled by anything. She would just lie down in the middle of the concert floor while the bands were testing their amps.

She just followed me wherever I went. On those nights when I knew I would be really busy and not spending much time at my desk, I would leave Vaida in the box office with whoever was working it that night. It always made me smile to hear the box-office folks excitedly say, "Yay! Vaida!" It made me smile even more when I would hear the customers say through the box-office window, "Oh my God, look at that cute dog in there!" She never really minded where she was, simply found a comfortable spot, curled up, and went to sleep.

I don't recall anyone ever having an issue with Vaida hanging around at Higher Ground. I worked at least five nights a week, but often it was six nights a week. She accompanied me at least three times a week over the course of the first four years of her life. Kevin and I have remained dear friends to this day, and when he recalled her first night there, he told me, "I think my voice either subdued her or scared her. But either way, she became part of the Higher Ground family that night. And always will be."

3

The Surgeries

For no reason other than my lease ending and my wanting to find a new and exciting, or sometimes cheaper, living situation, Vaida and I pretty much moved every year. My parents always joke that they can't even count all of the places I have lived since college. Between 2005 and 2019, it was twelve. It didn't seem like she was bothered by these moves. She always adjusted, and no landlord after meeting her for the first time ever refused to rent to me. As long as she had a comfortable place to sleep, she was content. The move from the farmhouse took me to Williston, Vermont, and a house with three other roommates. It was an awesome arrangement because I had the whole downstairs floor to myself. On those days when I had to leave Vaida home alone, my roommates would come down and play with her when they got home from work, but then they would go upstairs to where they lived, leaving her alone again.

This arrangement apparently didn't suit Vaida, as this was about the time she started to tear my stuff up while I was gone. This behavior came as quite a big surprise, given how well-behaved she'd been when left unattended at the farmhouse apartment where I'd lived alone. I began to wonder if hearing my roommates upstairs without being able to interact with them made her antsy, or if she had separation anxiety, was bored, or was just plain mad at me for leaving her home alone. Whatever it was made her chew and destroy my things. I would come home from work and find all sorts of things torn up. Usually it was something I didn't really need anyway, like books, mail, magazines, and record covers, but never anything important like an expensive pair of shoes. If I left any food around or within reach, she would most certainly get into it.

Probably the most concerning episode happened not when I was at work but when my mom came up for a visit. She and I were out doing errands. When we returned, I discovered that Vaida had somehow gotten into my backpack. I wouldn't ordinarily have cared about the chewed backpack, but I'd had back surgery two years earlier and had some prescription muscle relaxers in there for my occasional back pain. As soon as we came through the door, I saw my backpack on the floor, torn open, and the open medicine bottle lying next to it. I knew she must have eaten some of the pills. Alarmed, I called my vet. The vet said that dogs have to consume a million times—well, maybe not a million, but at least a considerable amount—more medication than the typical human dose to hurt them. Thankfully, Vaida was fine.

I wish I could say the same about Chips, my special teddy bear that I'd slept with every single night, tucked under my chin, ever since I got him in first grade. When I walked into the bedroom, Vaida was just lying there looking very innocent. Chips was on the floor not too far away with half his face gone. I was so mad and started crying, saying, "How could you do this to Chips?!" I was really, really mad at her. It was probably the maddest I have ever been at her throughout our entire relationship. I needed my teddy bear with me every night. I hadn't slept one night without Chips since the day I got him. Now half his face was missing.

Chips absolutely had to get repaired, and as soon as possible, so I reached out to the Vermont Teddy Bear Company. Unfortunately, they said they only repaired their own bears, but the person I spoke to was helpful enough to refer me to a woman in New York, just across Lake Champlain. I reached out and arranged to send Chips to her for repair.

When he came back, I was not happy because his face was very distorted and she used a different color fur for patching. Worse than that, his eyes were placed way too far apart, which completely changed his appearance. He was just not my Chips anymore. I couldn't help but cry when I saw him. He just didn't look right. I think I cried on and off for several days. There was no way I was keeping him like that. Sure, he still fit under my chin, but he was simply not the same old Chips.

After some online research, I was able to find a place in Chicago that did teddy bear repairs. Apparently, I wasn't the only person in need of bear repair because I wound up having to get an appointment and wait six long months to send him off for his "surgery." It seemed like a really cool place, run like a hospital for bears. Shortly after I sent him off, I started getting email updates, like, "Chips is getting prepared for surgery," or, "He just went into surgery," and, "I am pleased to tell you Chips's surgery went well and he is in recovery." When he came back, he even had his hospital wrist tag on and looked almost exactly the way I remembered him, or at least 90 to 95 percent back to normal. I still have that hospital tag in a memories box, and it always makes me laugh whenever I come across it and think to myself, *What a shitshow.*

I eventually got over being upset and mad at Vaida for what she did to Chips. Despite having owned him for over twenty years, he was, after all, a stuffed animal. Vaida was "my girl," my living, breathing constant companion. She brought me comfort and joy, and I believe I brought her the same. I finally realized that she was acting out because she simply missed me. In fact, it might not even have been me in particular that she missed, but just people in general. I truly believe that Vaida felt she was placed on this earth to bring comfort and joy to each and every life she touched. I decided that when I wasn't around, as long as someone else was there, she would be fine. She missed the company of people and the attention she got from them. I also accepted that if someone wasn't around, my stuff would probably get torn up.

Because Vaida was my first dog, I had to figure things out on my own in terms of her training and upbringing. I look back on it and joke that I used the "Big Daddy" approach to raising her.

I don't know if you're familiar with the Adam Sandler movie, *Big Daddy*, but it's a story about a young boy who shows up on Sandler's doorstep. Sandler is depicted as an immature and irresponsible guy with zero parenting skills who, due to circumstances out of his control, ends up having to care for the young boy. Sandler uses a hands-off approach and lets the boy name himself, dress himself, do whatever he wants, make his own way, and learn as he goes. Sandler does teach the boy a few "interesting" things, but not exactly what a parent would normally teach their kids—things like tripping roller-skaters, denting cans at the grocery store, and how to pee outside against a building. His approach apparently works because there is a scene where Sandler explains his method to his friend, "I let Frankenstein"—the name the boy gave himself—"decide what he wants to do. This is like a whole new school of child raising I'm doing. He makes his own decisions. You give the kid options instead of orders. Let him make the right decision." Sandler's friend then says to Frankenstein, "What do you want to do tomorrow?" Frankenstein replies, "I want to go to school." And Sandler replies, "Look at that. I don't force him. He makes the right decision."

It's probably a better parenting style for dogs than it would be for kids. I was lucky to have a dog who was mellow from day one and that this method worked. As Sandler did with Frankenstein, I let Vaida make her own way. I didn't force anything on her. I just kind of let her figure it out. She struck me as being really smart right from the very beginning. I would do things like leave her with a random person on the street while I ran into a store, or even walk down Church Street with her leash dragging along the ground. She always stayed right with me and never got excited or curious about anything or anyone around her whenever we were in public. I could leave her outside a store not even tied up, and she would just hang out until I came back. Obviously, if that wasn't working out, I wouldn't have continued to do that, but she adapted and was fine. I didn't do any formal training with her, and I never took her to doggie classes. My unusual training method seemed to be working.

A few months after I got her, in the fall of 2010, I got an opportunity to scratch something off my bucket list. I'd always wanted to go on the road with a band, and that chance came when I was invited to go on tour with Grace Potter and the Nocturnals. Grace Potter is a recording artist from Vermont. She and her band were about to go on a two-month tour across the country and needed somebody to manage their merchandise sales. I had become friends with Grace and the band members through working at Higher Ground. Benny, her guitarist, who knew me quite well, suggested they bring me along. How could I turn that down?

With Kevin's blessing, I went on tour and Vaida went on vacation to my parents' house. My parents had a dog at that time, so sending Vaida to live with them would not be a problem. My mom was much stricter, however, when it came to training. I jokingly called it Mom's Boot Camp for Vaida. My mom had a trainer she was using for her dog, and since Vaida was going to be there for two months, she insisted Vaida join in. Although Vaida hadn't destroyed anything else that was important or meaningful to me since the Chips incident, she was still occasionally chewing random belongings of mine. We thought this would be the perfect opportunity to work on this behavior. Crate training may have seemed like the obvious solution, but I couldn't bear the thought of her being cooped up in a cage whenever she had to be left alone while my parents were at work. Plus, I knew as soon as I got back, Vaida's alone time would be limited since we were generally always together.

My mom kept a journal so I could read about her stay when I got back. She came home every day at lunchtime to check on the dogs and let them out. On some days all was well. Other days weren't so great. Vaida sometimes found something to get into, like the mail or a magazine, but as usual, nothing really important. Any food in her reach was also fair game, but my mom quickly learned how to Vaida-proof the house to limit the damage.

I don't know if it was necessarily the training and the time spent at boot camp, or just the fact that Vaida's behavior improved with age, but thankfully, her destructive behaviors lasted a year at the most, maybe not even that long. I definitely think as she got older, she adjusted to my schedule and learned her mom, me, would always come back home.

After spending a year living in the house with the three roommates, it was time to move again. This time, Vaida and I moved in with a co-worker from Higher Ground to a great A-frame-style house by a beautiful lake tucked in the woods of Hinesburg, Vermont. If I wasn't taking her for a hike up a mountain, we were going for a long walk on the dirt roads in our neighborhood and a swim after.

Very quickly, all of my neighbors knew and loved Vaida and would come out to greet us whenever they spotted us walking down the road. As time went on, my neighbors started asking me, "Caitlin, what's wrong with Vaida?" This was also starting to happen when I was out in public with her. Strangers began to ask me, "What's wrong with your dog?"

Apparently Vaida was limping, and I hadn't noticed. It took multiple people telling me they noticed her limp before I finally recognized it. Because so many people had been mentioning it to me, on one walk in particular, I purposely ran ahead of her and recorded her strolling toward me. I could see that she was limping, but I didn't want to admit it because that could mean she might not be able to do things with me. I kept an eye on it, and when the limp didn't go away, I realized she needed to be seen. I made an appointment with my vet in Hinesburg.

On the day of the appointment, I was nervous as I drove to the office. I had no idea what to expect. When the vet asked me what was going on with her, I described her limp and showed him the recording but said she really didn't seem to be too bothered by it. With Vaida lying in the exam room, I anxiously watched as he pulled on, yanked, and stretched her left front leg. She just lay there and let him do it.

I said, "See, she's fine. No big deal."

He said, "Caitlin, I think I know what's wrong. There's one thing I'm going to do to her that she might react to because she hasn't reacted to anything else I've done. Don't worry, I will try not to really hurt her." He pulled her front left elbow a certain way, and she let out a very quiet yelp.

X-rays confirmed his suspicion that she had a very small bone chip in her elbow. I don't honestly recall what the vet said in regard to why this happened, but I suspect it was either from overuse at such a young age or perhaps how quickly she had grown.

She had to have surgery to have the bone chip removed. A specialist, who was one of the best veterinary surgeons in Vermont, was called in to perform the surgery a few weeks later. The surgery went well and without any complications. Postoperative instructions included keeping her quiet and super mellow, both easily accomplished, and no hiking for six weeks, which was not so easy.

It was right before summer, and I couldn't take her hiking with me. I had to adjust my summer plans. Because my house was literally on the shores of a beautiful lake, I decided that this six-week recovery period wasn't going to be that big of a deal. We could just hang out in the yard and I could read or relax while Vaida lounged nearby. I also remember that the surgical site, and in fact most of her left leg and shoulder area, had to be shaved down to the skin. That presented the perfect canvas for me to give Vaida my version of a tattoo. With a red and a black Sharpie marker, I drew a heart with an arrow and "Mom" in the middle. She had that for quite a few days until the ink wore off.

After four weeks of no exercise and hanging out by the lake with me, she seemed like she had made a full recovery. The vet was pleased with her healing and deemed the surgery a success. Although I shouldn't admit this, I definitely took her on a few "short-ish" hikes before the full six weeks was up. Just like an active person would be getting antsy after being bedridden for so long, Vaida was probably desiring activity herself. I know I was. After being laid up for several weeks, Vaida and I resumed our normal hiking adventures.

4

"Must Be Willing to Thrive in a Dog-Friendly Environment"

I had worked for Higher Ground Concert Hall for eight years when I decided it was time for a change. I needed something different from the late-night hours that working in the music industry required. I didn't have any sort of job in mind and was open to any and all possibilities. Craigslist always had interesting job postings, so I started my search there. I was looking for places that specialized in things I liked, so I started typing words in the search bar like "bread," "cheese," and "dogs." Maybe I'd work in a bakery or learn how to make cheese, or maybe I'd get really lucky and find a job where Vaida could come with me.

Vermont is a small state with a lot of cool, small, locally owned businesses. I was sure I'd be able to find a job at one of them. Typing "dogs" in the search bar led me to a position that offered full-time hours seasonally, located about ninety minutes south of where I was living. The job was picking, packing, and shipping orders in a high-volume warehouse. One of the things that caught my eye was the statement, "must be willing to thrive in a dog-friendly environment." How perfect was that?

The name of the company was Ibex Outdoor Clothing. I'd never heard of them, so I went on their website and saw that they made really high-end merino wool clothing and allowed their employees to bring their dogs to work. They even had a page dedicated to their pets, where the dogs' pictures, names, and their owners' names were displayed. I was blown away.

Ibex was started by a gentleman named John Fernsell in Woodstock, Vermont, in 1997. He was a dog lover, and his dog Shak was named after the famous explorer Ernest Shackleton. Ibex also had a garment named the "Shak," a long-sleeve pullover that was one of its most popular garments. Ibex was a place that brought canines and people together. This was the culture that John and his wife, Jineese, created and wanted to continue. Ibex didn't just sell high-end merino wool clothing. Ibex created and supported a lifestyle for its employees, one that included the love and companionship of pets.

After thoroughly perusing their website, I called my mom and said, "You've got to hear this," and I read her the job description. The only thing was that Ibex was located in White River Junction, which would mean yet another move. Being so far from all of the mountains and places Vaida and I had come to love, I wasn't thrilled about the location but knew I had to apply. The idea of bringing Vaida to work with me every day just sounded too good to pass up. I applied and got hired as soon as I interviewed. Vaida and I moved again.

Because I wanted to be sure that Vaida could come to work with me, I made sure to mention her during my interview. I said to Jonathan, the warehouse manager who was interviewing me, "I have a dog and I would like to bring her to work with me." Jonathan said the position was in the warehouse and although they allowed dogs in the offices, he wasn't sure that dogs would be allowed in the warehouse, or that it would be safe to do so. His many concerns were things like she might pee in there or wander off because the doors were often open for deliveries, or she might get in the way of warehouse equipment, or simply get lost in the massive space.

Clearly, he didn't know Vaida. I said, "Trust me, I can bring my dog to the warehouse. She is going to sleep the entire day. She's not going to wander around. She's not going to bother anyone. She's not going to get in the way of a forklift."

Jonathan agreed that we could give it a try.

I was lucky to find a new place to live relatively quickly and started work one week after the interview. I didn't bring Vaida with me right away. I wanted to get the hang of the job before I brought her along. My job was to grab a stack of orders, walk up and down the aisles and "pick" all of the product to be shipped, and then bring them to the shipping station at the front of the warehouse. Sometimes I would hand the products off to a shipper to sort into the individual orders, and other times I would do the shipping myself.

Once I got the hang of things and knew she would be safe there, I started bringing Vaida with me every day. She often stayed up front with me when I worked the shipping station. Directly under the counter where I worked were some good-sized cubbies, which made a perfect spot for Vaida to sleep, especially after I laid a blanket down for her. When I spent my days picking the products from the warehouse aisles, she stayed up front with whoever was shipping, snuggled and snoozing away in her cubby.

You hardly even knew there was a dog in the ten-thousand-square-foot warehouse. She never got up. She never looked for me. The warehouse activity never bothered her, not even when the pickers and packers tossed large baskets of clothing across the floor toward the empty shipping boxes where she lay. She wouldn't so much as flinch. She also was not bothered by the comings and goings of all the delivery trucks, not even when they backed into the building through the doors at the front of the huge warehouse. Vaida never got scared of the trucks or got in their way. She just hung out all day. It was so cool to come back from picking orders to find her in her cubby or resting on the cold cement among all of the busy shippers. We always had loud rock music playing over the speakers, so maybe that helped her feel right at home in this new workplace. It was noisy, loud, and busy, just like at Higher Ground.

Sometimes Vaida would get up and wander outside through the open warehouse doors and find a grassy spot or other comfy place to sleep. She liked to lie under one particular pickup truck, and the owner knew that and always checked Vaida's whereabouts before taking off. Other times she'd hang out for a little bit in the sun or take herself into the woods to do her business. Then she'd come right back and go to sleep.

If Vaida got bored or tired of the warehouse activity, her solution was to find her way to the back of the warehouse where the returns department was located. They had a door that led directly into the warehouse, so Vaida would let out one single quiet bark at the door and one of the staff would let her in. Sometimes if I was in an aisle near the returns department, I could hear them exclaim, "Yay! Vaida's here." Once inside, she'd curl up on one of the dog beds in there and resume sleeping. I thought it was really cute that Vaida figured out how to take a break from the warehouse chaos and find some peace and quiet in the returns department.

In addition to being sweet and mellow, Vaida was also very smart. She quickly learned that at four thirty the FedEx truck would be coming by to pick up the day's shipping orders. This truck always backed into the warehouse doorway, beeping the entire time it was in reverse. Knowing that the driver, Paul, always brought treats, Vaida could be dead to the world, snoring, sound asleep, but as soon as she heard the familiar *beep, beep, beep*, she'd wake up and run right over to the truck, patiently waiting out of the way until Paul emerged and gave her a treat. It was the sweetest thing to watch.

Ibex had about fifty employees during the busy summer months and typically anywhere from fifteen to twenty dogs on-site. One of the seasonal warehouse employees had a dog that he brought into work a few times, but Vaida was the only dog in the warehouse on a full-time basis. In fact, she was the first dog ever in the warehouse. It was a year or two later when another dog joined the warehouse crew. Her name was Maggie, and she was the sweetest little black mutt. She was Vaida's age but less than half her size. She liked to nap and snooze with Vaida in the cubby. Vaida liked it too because Maggie's back was a great place for her to rest her chin. It was an adorable sight. Vaida took the lead and showed Maggie how to be a warehouse dog. She showed her how to stay out of the way and to relax all day, but most importantly, she taught Maggie about the FedEx truck and the daily treats.

Because of several "incidents," within a few months of my starting at Ibex, management decided to create a dog committee and make a few rules. One rule was that your dog had to stay at your desk. When you came in and out of the building, your dog had to be on a leash, and you definitely had to pick up after them. The dog committee also adopted a three-strike rule. If the dog did anything wrong, like get into a fight or scuffle with another dog, they'd get a strike. Three strikes and they were kicked out. If someone had a complaint about a dog, they could talk to a member of the dog committee and the dog committee would address it. Thankfully for all of us, the dogs at Ibex were well-behaved (for the most part), so the committee never had to kick a dog out.

While still working as a seasonal employee, I was moved into a full-time permanent position, and a year after that, I was promoted to assistant manager of the warehouse. It could have been because of my strong work ethic, but I wouldn't be surprised if it was simply because everyone loved Vaida so much and wanted her to stick around. I worked as assistant manager for a year when management asked me to take over the returns department, so I left the warehouse. It was a smaller space, but Vaida didn't seem to mind. As long as she had a place to sleep, she was happy. In the spring and summer, we would open the double doors that led out to the back parking lot, and she was free to come and go. Even though Vaida was now in the returns department, separate from the warehouse and far from the delivery area, she still figured out how to go see Paul. At four thirty, she would hear the FedEx truck's familiar *beep, beep, beep* and run (at Vaida speed) out of the open back doors and all the way around three sides of the building to go collect her treat. If the back doors weren't open, she would wake up and go to the door that led to the warehouse and let out one quiet bark for someone to open it so she could go through the warehouse to see Paul.

One time, before I took over the returns department, Denise, the returns manager, brought her cat to work. She thought that if everyone could bring their dog, she should be able to bring her cat. She made a little cat cubby in a closet. Three hours into the cat being there, HR found out and sent Denise and her cat home. I'm not exactly sure why, but that was against the rules. I'm guessing Ibex chose to limit it to strictly dogs because if Denise's cat was allowed to stay, next thing you know, folks would be bringing in all sorts of pets. I didn't notice any dogs reacting to the cat, but it was funny to watch the revolving door of employees walking into the returns department laughing and peeking their heads into the cat's closet. It made for a very entertaining morning at work.

A few weeks later, Vaida and I got sent home too. That morning before we left for work, Vaida got skunked. I quickly gave her a bath, but she still smelled really bad. I didn't want to leave her in my house to stink it up, so I brought her to work like I always did. It took less than an hour for me and Vaida to get sent home. Bringing a smelly dog to work was against the rules too.

Most of the dogs that came to work were purebred and larger dogs. Shak was a golden retriever. John and Jineese also had this really cool clumber spaniel, a breed I'd never heard of. Clumbers are bigger spaniels and really unique-looking. I loved their clumber named Izzi. There were also some Labs and some Irish Setters, along with a boxer. There were small dogs too. There was a beagle, a Boston terrier, and the woman in customer service had a cute little Pomeranian named Crumpet. The main entrance into most of the offices was through the warehouse, and Crumpet knew the warehouse manager had treats, so every morning she'd go skittering across the cement floor and straight to his desk, looking for her treat. It was the cutest thing. She would stand up on her hind legs and wave her little paws, and Brian would dangle the treat in front of her face so she'd have to stretch and reach for it. Of course, Vaida would wake up, slowly walk over, and wait for her treat too.

There were at least fifteen, sometimes as many as twenty dogs that came to work at Ibex on an average day. Some people brought two dogs. When I first started, it was mostly older, mature dogs, not puppies. After a few years, there was a puppy explosion. Everyone was getting puppies. It was insane.

For the most part, the dogs were pretty calm, but when "puppy mania" happened, it got pretty wild. The increase in puppies at work brought about changes in the rules. Puppies had to be at least six months old and have some basic obedience skills before they were allowed to be at work.

Some of my fondest memories of my time at Ibex centered around Vaida and her relationships with my coworking family. The warehouse manager was a really cool guy named Brian, who taught Vaida to whisper instead of bark for a treat. He didn't have a dog, but he really loved Vaida.

When she was young, I'd taught her to "speak." I'd say, "Vaida, speak," and she'd "woof" in her normal dog voice. Brian decided that he didn't want her to do that, that he wanted her to be quieter and whisper instead. Rather than saying, "Speak," he would say, "Whisper," and put his finger to his lips. She would make a movement with her mouth like she was barking, but no sound came out. All you had to do was put your finger in front of your lips and say, "shhh," and she would just move her mouth with no sound coming out. I'm not sure how long it took Brian to teach her that. Frankly, I literally have no idea how he got her to do it at all.

After learning this great new trick, I could even get her to go back and forth. I'd get her to whisper, and then say "speak" kind of loud, and she would bark in her normal dog voice. It was really impressive. Vaida was not a beggar by any means, but I think she liked her whisper trick so much that if you were eating something and she decided she wanted a bite, she would just move her mouth to whisper, having learned this got a big reaction from people. It was the darnedest, cutest thing.

Vaida and I both enjoyed interacting with our coworkers and their dogs outside of the Ibex walls as well. A group of us often went to Hurricane Park, a quiet spot a short two-minute drive from Ibex that had a couple of miles of trails in the woods and a pond.

My friend Cathy organized these outings. She had a dog named Shilo, a shepherd mix with a lot of energy, who liked to go for walks. When Cathy sent an email to all of the dog owners in the company that said, "Dog walk at lunch," anyone who had the time would drive over to Hurricane Park and we'd head to the trails. It was usually six or eight of us with six or eight dogs, walking and talking as we let the dogs run. It was really fun, and I think the dogs enjoyed it as much as we did.

Most of the dogs ran back and forth and up and down the trail, playing with each other. Vaida, on the other hand, just ambled along with the humans. Long recovered from her elbow surgery, this simply was her pace. She wasn't very interested in the other dogs. It didn't matter how many other dogs were around. If she wanted to lie down, she lay down. If she was hiking, she hiked. She just wanted to be with the people and go at a normal pace with everyone else. She got along with the other dogs of Ibex, but she just didn't interact with them as much as she did with the people. I'm convinced she thought she was a human.

In the summer, we had an extended lunch break once a week called Take Time Thursday. On this day we got an hour and a half break designed to get us all outside together. The extra time meant we could go on longer walks or hikes or go to the river and paddle board and let the dogs swim. Yet another perk of working at this awesome company.

Ibex was not only dog friendly but was made up of very like-minded outdoor people. Sometimes one of the employees would organize post-work bike rides. In the winter, there were prework ski adventures at a local ski hill called Suicide Six. We'd meet there before the lifts opened, attach skins to the bottoms of our skis, and hike up the mountain, then we'd ski down. I only went a couple times because I was terrible at skiing. I don't remember if any other dogs went, but Vaida always came along. She liked the mountains at any time.

One of the best things about having Vaida at work with me was that we could go for a short hike or a walk nearly every single day on our commute home. One place we loved to go after work was Lucy's Lookout in Woodstock, Vermont, which was a really beautiful spot right off the Appalachian Trail. Lucy's Lookout has a little cabin that hikers can use even though it's not an official A.T. shelter. The hike to the lookout was just a few miles long, but it was a great way to relax and decompress after work. Once we got to the lookout, Vaida would relax in the grass while I climbed up a ladder that lead to a deck on the roof of the cabin to enjoy the 360-degree view of the area. We loved going there after work, not only because it was basically on the way home but because we got to spend time on the A.T. and wind down.

Making the change from my irregular night schedule at Higher Ground to Ibex, where I had two days off in a row for the first time, exposed me to a whole new world of possibilities. When I realized that, at five on Friday evening, I didn't have to be back to work until nine on Monday morning, that really motivated me to spend a lot of time outdoors with Vaida. Everyone at Ibex knew that every weekend Vaida and I were off on some outside adventure. Spring, summer, and fall were spent hiking the higher elevation mountains and winters were spent snowshoeing and going on shorter hikes. On Fridays, my coworkers would ask me what we were going to do that weekend. On Mondays, they would ask me what mountains we climbed or what our adventure had been. Most of the people working at Ibex shared a passion for the outdoors, whether it was hiking, biking, rock climbing, or skiing. I loved sharing stories and talking about our experiences after the weekend.

Spending all of our time on Vermont mountains, it wasn't until three years into working at Ibex that we hiked in New Hampshire for the first time and also went on our first official winter hike. New Hampshire has forty-eight mountains that are over four thousand feet, and Vaida and I hadn't even begun to scratch the surface. In March of 2015, my co-worker Michael invited us along with two other coworkers to hike one of the 48, Mount Moosilauke. Being that it was about an hour's drive from where we lived in Vermont and the closest four-thousand-footer to us, it quickly became our favorite. It was this hike with coworkers that opened up the doors for us to start exploring the New Hampshire 48 and recognize that I no longer had to limit my hiking to three seasons. It is because of our time spent at Ibex that Vaida and I developed into experienced and accomplished four-season hikers.

5

Becoming Famous

When I accepted the job at Ibex after responding to the craigslist ad requiring a willingness to thrive in a dog-friendly atmosphere, I knew I would be entering an environment filled with dog lovers but didn't know it would be an environment comprised of such like-minded outdoor enthusiasts. I had no idea I would be entering a community that would provide me the opportunity to flourish and grow as a hiker and as a person. I was still quiet and shy. Especially in the beginning when I was still trying to find my comfort zone with people. I just assumed I would continue my standard hiking alone with just my best friend Vaida by my side. Within the first few weeks of working at Ibex, coworkers started to catch on to just how avid a hiker I was and how adventurous Vaida and I were. I could no longer hide alone in the aisles of the warehouse or out on the trail. My coworkers wanted to hear about our adventures. The more Vaida and I did, the more people wanted to hear about it. Most of the folks working there had stories to tell after their weekends, but soon Vaida and I were expected to have stories to tell after our weekends too. We became *the* hikers. Gaining this notoriety afforded us the opportunity to be featured in a variety of videos and articles. (See VAIDA ON THE WEB AND IN THE PRESS in the back of this book to view them.)

One of the most exciting things that happened was when the company won Purina's national "Pets at Work" contest, which had been designed to celebrate pet-friendly companies across the United States. Contestants were required to explain how pets make a positive impact on the workplace and why the workday is better for employees and their pets. Contestants also had to describe the company's Pets at Work program and provide three to five photos that showed pets in their workplace.

I'll never forget the day I learned about the contest. It was just a few months after I started working at Ibex. I was talking with a couple of my coworkers as we were busy packing shipments, joking with one of them in particular, making fun of him for living with his parents.

He said, "I was hanging out with my folks, and we were watching the National Dog Show. We saw a commercial by Purina about a contest they were running for the country's most pet-friendly company."

Immediately I said, "Holy shit, that is amazing. We have to enter!"

Everyone's response was, "Okay, Caitlin, who is going to do that? Who is going to take the time to jump through all those hoops?"

I kept saying, "Someone's got to do it. We've got to find someone." So I ran upstairs to marketing and told them that Purina was running this contest.

They said, "That's cool, Caitlin, but we've got a lot on our plates."

I couldn't believe they weren't interested. I ran over to my friend Brian in the production department.

He thought it was cool and agreed we should enter and that he would create the submission if he got the green light from Melissa in HR, but was busy and couldn't do it right away.

It was December, and we had to get our entry in by the end of January, so I told him, "I'll keep reminding you. I won't remind you every day, but I will every other day." Even though I was a brand-new employee and didn't feel I carried much clout, I was bound and determined to get us entered into the contest. So, every other day, I said, "Brian, have you sent in the entry yet?"

Five days before it was due, he sent in the letter. It was a great letter. He described Ibex perfectly when he said:

Ibex headquarters couldn't be described as dog friendly; dog obsessed might be more accurate. The smiling face, wagging tail, and wet kisses that most people expect at home, or highly anticipate at the end of a long workday, are available to us all day, every day at work. Most importantly, having our dogs alongside us at work helps us maintain a healthy and happy work-life balance, an oft-overlooked and difficult-to-achieve accomplishment in this busy world.

March came and went without hearing anything, and my enthusiasm for winning began to dwindle. A month later, Melissa held a company meeting for all of the employees and their dogs. Vaida was probably snoring during the whole meeting. Purina had selected Ibex to be in the top five nominees for the contest. This was really exciting news, and my enthusiasm returned. I couldn't believe something I'd initiated actually put us in the running.

Melissa told us that Actor John O'Hurley, well-known for his role as J. Peterman on the TV show *Seinfeld* and host of Purina's National Dog Show, was going to be choosing the winning entry.

A month later, we had another company-wide meeting and it was announced that we had won! I thought to myself, *We did it! I can't believe we actually did it! Ibex is the most pet-friendly workplace in the country.*

Our prize included John O'Hurley coming to our headquarters to present us with a check for ten thousand dollars to donate to a local humane society. Purina also gave Ibex five thousand dollars to make the facility more dog friendly. If Ibex had owned the building, we could have really "dog-friendlified" it, maybe even building an outdoor play area. The dog committee took charge of the prize money and right off the bat bought dog treats and leashes, pooper scoopers, and dog beds.

The other really cool part of the prize was that they sent a film crew from Los Angeles to do a story on Ibex as well as a feature on three employees and their dogs. Anyone who was interested in being selected had to fill out a submission form and talk about themselves and their dog(s). Obviously, I was interested. I felt like I had the best dog ever and really hoped they would pick Vaida and me. She was so cool, and I was, after all, the one who'd kept prodding Ibex until they got it done. But also, as soon as they saw pictures of Vaida and heard about her adventurous life, I figured it was kind of a no-brainer. And I was right.

Vaida and I, along with two coworkers and their dogs, were selected, and the film crew spent three days filming us at Ibex and at each of our houses. The idea was to see how these employees lived and worked with their dogs, to see their home environment and what they did with their dogs outside of work.

I lived in East Barnard, a little dirt-road community in Vermont, in a house built in the 1800s that used to be the town's general store. It was located right on a brook, perfect for swimming. The film crew spent an afternoon interviewing me at my house and were excited when they heard about our hiking adventures. They were hoping to go for an actual hike with us, but we ran out of time. Instead, they did some filming around my house and dirt-road neighborhood. Vaida loved to swim, so they filmed her swimming in the brook right in my backyard. The video footage was edited into a one-minute video about Vaida and me. I don't think it was ever actually a commercial on TV, but it looked like one. I don't honestly know what it was even used for. It ends with the words on the screen, "Pets and people are better together." I couldn't agree more. I'm not sure I thought about it or realized it at the time, but what a memory this video created for me. It truly captured my relationship with Vaida and will forever hold a special place in my heart. In those moments when I find myself really missing Vaida, I will pull up that video and it always seems to make me smile.

The film crew also produced a three-minute video about the pet-friendly culture at Ibex and how it brought canines and people together. I often watch this video when I'm missing not only Vaida but the Ibex family and my time spent there. I miss that place so much.

Somehow the pet-friendly culture at Ibex caught the attention of NBC Nightly News with Lester Holt. NBC sent Harry Smith to do a story about it, focusing on the fact that working at Ibex provided a perk you generally could not get anywhere else—being able to spend your entire day with your four-legged best friend. While I didn't appear in the video, Vaida got to lie in Harry Smith's lap as he narrated the news story. Vaida on national TV. How cool was that?

One of the longest video shoots that Vaida and I were featured in was created by Ibex and Osprey, a well-known backpack company. It was to be a collaborative photo and video shoot where Osprey was planning to get photos for a new super ultralightweight backpack that they were coming out with and Ibex was going to create an inspirational video about the hiking community. Knowing that I was a very active member of the hiking community and had the unique distinction of always hiking with my ninety-pound dog, Evan, Ibex's photo and video marketing lead, asked me if Vaida and I wanted to step out of the office for a few days to be in the shoot. It would feature Vaida, my boyfriend Jodeob, and me using the Osprey packs and Ibex gear. Because of my knowledge of the White Mountains of New Hampshire, I was also asked to plan most of the shoot, what to do and where to go. It was kind of fun. This was their gig, but I was going to make up the adventure.

Because the trip was taking place in the White Mountains, I told them about a friend I had who owned a hostel in the Whites and about a gentleman named Carl, better known as "The Omelette Guy," in order for them to get creative content for the video story. I planned hikes to Artist Bluff and an overnight in the Northern Presidentials in order to get some shots of the gear in use in really rugged and beautiful terrain.

There were two videos that resulted from the Osprey partnership. The first focused on Vaida, Jodeob, and me as we talked about the benefits of ultralight backpacking. I described my dream day as waking up at dawn, starting to hike, spending the whole day covering a large number of miles until we're too tired to go on, and then setting up camp wherever we land. I was lucky that Vaida was such a trooper and able to do the big miles with me. This style of backpacking is totally different from going on overnight hikes with specific campsite goals in mind. I also talked about the benefits of ultralight backpacking, which help me accomplish my hiking goals on these long days. Certainly, it was a promo video for Osprey's products, but it fit us so well.

The second video that resulted from the partnership was specifically about Carl, The Omelette Guy. Evan thought that was such an intriguing story for Osprey, and Osprey did too, so they ended up doing the story. Carl had a full-blown cooking setup on the Appalachian Trail in the middle of the woods. It was a huge tarp system set up with two-by-fours, complete with a workstation, serving counter, chairs, and coolers. The kitchen setup was left there permanently every night, along with the chairs, water, and even five-gallon buckets with any leftover bananas or snacks for the latecomers. I had met him the previous year when I was hiking a section of the Appalachian Trail with Jodeob. We'd stumbled upon his outdoor kitchen in the woods, where he provided hot food, bananas, cookies, beverages, and whatever else he had on hand that day, to the hikers who came, and it was all free. Carl said that every year at least 1,400 hikers would stop by for food, drinks, or help. He insisted that you ate as much as you could. He told us the largest omelet he'd ever served was made with thirty eggs.

Vaida, Jodeob, and I are prominently featured in that video along with numerous other hikers. It describes Carl's "trail magic," which is defined as "acts of generosity in wild and primitive settings of the Appalachian Trail—where basic amenities of civilization are intentionally absent."

It's an inspiring story of a retired man who sets up his omelet station every day for people hiking the Appalachian Trail. He never runs out of food, and he willingly and happily gives you as much as you can eat. He says, "This is your Social Security dollars at work."

Carl was too busy cooking omelets for a handful of hungry hikers, so he didn't get to interact with Vaida much, but the reason I included this video is not just because Vaida and I are featured in it in several spots. I included it because it describes the hiking community in the White Mountains and along the Appalachian Trail. Carl talks about how people on the trail don't want to take the last cookie or eat as much as they can because they want to save some for the next person on the trail. That's the culture of hikers.

Back in 2016, the year Vaida and I completed the NH48, we were in the White Mountains every single weekend, year-round. The more we hiked together, the more I learned about what to do and what not to do when hiking with my dog. I learned to carry only those things in my pack that were absolutely necessary to maintain my and Vaida's safety and needs while on trail. I even got Vaida her own custom pack so she could carry her own supplies. I don't know where I got the idea or what prompted me to even consider writing an article about our experiences together on trail, but that's exactly what I did. When the idea struck, GearJunkie.com was the obvious choice. It is a highly trafficked website among outdoor enthusiasts, who are able to contribute articles for publication on the site. I wrote an article, they accepted it, and I got paid for doing it. I wrote other articles as well, but the most relevant to this book, of course, is the one about hiking with Vaida. It was instructional on how to prepare your dog to be your hiking companion.

The Green Mountain Club is the founder and maintainer of the Long Trail, the oldest long-distance trail in America. As part of their oversight of the Long Trail, they provide certificates of completion and patches to those who hike all 273 miles of Vermont's Long Trail. I don't normally care about lists, accomplishments, or the patches and certificates that go along with them; however, the Long Trail was my first long-distance hiking adventure with Vaida. In order to get the certificate and patch and become a certified "End-to-Ender," I had to submit a written account of the hike. I didn't keep a journal while I was actively hiking the trail, but I took lots of pictures. I didn't submit my report until a couple of months after I finished. To be honest, I probably did it right at the deadline at the end of the year. Even though some time had passed, it was an adventure I'll never forget. Going back and looking at all of the pictures I took helped me to specifically recall our time on the trail in great detail. I also had a phone app that most long-distance hikers use, called Guthook (recently renamed to FarOut) that shows mileage, elevation, profile, and maps. After looking at that, I could easily recall what I did each day and created a blog journaling our adventure. Vaida and I got our first official certificate and patch.

I started at Ibex in August 2012. Sadly, they closed their doors, liquidated the property, and sold the company in the fall of 2017. A few employees, including me, were asked to stay on a little longer to help with the remaining closing tasks. My final day there was in February of 2018, Ibex's last day ever. After we liquidated and all said goodbye, Ibex has since been reborn and you can still find them online. They are now being operated under new ownership on a much smaller scale in Colorado.

I loved working there so much. Getting to bring Vaida to work with me every day was a huge bonus, and for those five-and-a-half years, it was simply an incredible place to work. I felt like I spent every single day with family. Being surrounded by so many inspiring and like-minded people, and the incredible culture at Ibex contributed to my personal growth and solidified the strong bond that Vaida and I had already started. We entered Ibex as a girl and her dog who liked hiking and emerged as a confident woman and her veteran four-legged hiking companion, an inseparable duo obsessed with hiking and backpacking. To this day, I can hear the sound of the shuffle of Vaida's big paws slowly walking along the warehouse cement. Ibex was where I would have worked forever.

6

"You're Coming with Me, Vaida"

Vaida was my constant companion. We were always together, whether at work, out doing errands, or hiking. She was an extension of me. A part of me. Something I rarely had to think about as far as needs or wants. In fact, I never felt like I *needed* to do anything for her. Anything I did for Vaida was already part of my daily routine or something I wanted to do. Going to the pet store to buy crunchies was a fun outing because we got to meet other pet lovers and have a conversation. I *liked* taking her to the vet. It was something I looked forward to because the vet loved her so much. So did the front desk people. I was proud to walk into the waiting room and have the other pet owners "ooh" and "ahh" over her manners as well as her beauty.

It didn't take long for me to understand that ours was a bond greater than normal between a human and a pet. It was almost as if she shared my interests and wanted to be a part of them. She seemed so content when she was with me. I sensed this pretty much as soon as I adopted her. I'm convinced a large part of it was that she simply wanted to be with me. So, no matter what we did, I could almost hear her thinking, *I guess that's what we're doing today.*

I could take Vaida everywhere with me. Outdoor concerts, firework displays, farmers' markets, outdoor food and beer festivals, parades.

Places where hundreds, if not thousands, of people gathered. And it made me feel proud to show her off and watch her attract attention and draw random conversations from strangers. I never felt like I couldn't go somewhere I wanted, like a friend's house for dinner or a party, because she just came along. Once we got to where we were going the most exciting thing that would happen would be Vaida finding a comfortable place to sleep. People naturally gravitated toward her, and before I knew it, she was making new friends. Often, I would be told I should make her a therapy dog because of the calming presence and comfort she brought people. I truly do believe Vaida thought she was a human.

We always made it a point to get out and be active. Some days it was just walking around on Church Street, the pedestrian retail street in downtown Burlington. Other days, we'd go for walks or on a nearby hike. On warmer days, we'd find a place for Vaida to swim. If she wasn't out and about with me, she lounged. When she tired of that, she did her other favorite thing—she slept. She wasn't the kind of dog that had to be up and moving around and entertained.

The first three years of Vaida's life, I worked nights at Higher Ground, and on the nights that she didn't come to work with me and I got home in the middle of the night or early morning, I'd find her lying on my bed or the couch with her head on a pillow. I'd open the door, she'd turn her head, look at me, and then put her head right back down and close her eyes. She didn't get up to greet me. She probably had been sleeping the whole time and was anxious to get back to it.

I'm not really sure what dictated which evenings I would bring Vaida to Higher Ground with me. Maybe I didn't have time to drop her off after that day's hike, maybe it was a mellow acoustic show she could watch a bit of, maybe I had friends coming who I knew would want to see her, or maybe I just really wanted my best friend with me that night. It didn't matter what was going on at Higher Ground that night, how busy, loud, or hectic it was. She would just sleep at my desk.

One of the best parts of having Vaida with me at work was coming back to my desk and seeing her there. I loved being able to pet her and get love from her in the middle of my work shift. I also loved seeing how much joy she brought to others, whether it was my coworkers, patrons, or the bands that were playing. Getting ready for shows was always chaotic, but because of her calming presence, I think it helped put other folks in the right frame of mind for the night. Everyone seemed to love having her around, and that made me feel good.

If I was having a bad day, Vaida was my coping mechanism when I got stressed. Seeing her gentle face and just having her close by soothed me. Sometimes, when I needed a break from the chaos, I would lie on the floor with her for a few minutes. Sometimes I would catch my co-workers doing the same. I really *should* have made her a therapy dog. I think some dogs have the ability to know their purpose is to love and to bring smiles and calm, and that certainly described Vaida.

Vaida was also able to bring a sense of calm to my mom. She often said, "I can't believe you're hiking alone." My response would always be, "I'm not alone. I have Vaida." If something happened to me on the trail, maybe she couldn't save me the way a human could, but she'd be right there with me and I truly believed that she would have tried to do something. Luckily, I never had to experience that.

Vaida never gave any sign that she didn't want to come everywhere with me. She was my shadow, my partner. I called her, and she came. I'm not sure what I would have done if she didn't want to be with me, especially on my frequent hikes. If she truly didn't want to go, I probably would have left her at home. But her not wanting to join me on the hikes never came up. As soon as I opened the car door, she got right out and headed straight to the trail.

Vaida didn't hike like other dogs I saw on trails, running ahead, running back, running off trail, chasing after wildlife. Right from the very first time we hiked together, she took the lead about ten feet ahead and simply ambled along. When she saw people up ahead on the trail taking a snack or water break, she would calmly wander over and literally sit down next to them. I could always tell when she ran into other hikers because I could hear the excited voices of people ahead of me saying, "Oh my God, look at this beautiful dog!" Yup, that was my dog, my beautiful girl, Vaida. She didn't paw them, get in their faces, or bother them in any way. Seeing her politely sitting with complete strangers made me feel good, and I suspect by her look of contentment that it made her feel good too.

When we got to the summit of whatever mountain we hiked that day, I was always amazed at what she did next. She would wander a little bit away from where I was standing and find a spot to sit and stare at the view. It was like she was reveling in her accomplishment and taking it all in, almost like a queen surveying her kingdom. And then she lay down.

Hiking was definitely in Vaida's comfort zone. I never saw any sign from her that we had hiked too much, or not enough. I never noticed a change in her behavior. She was just as happy hanging out and doing nothing as she was happy to come with me. After a long day on trail, she parked herself on her bed, her Mutt Mat, the couch, or the floor in the exact same way she would had she been lounging all day and just come inside from doing her business. It's interesting, she would be content not going on a hike for three or four days in a row, but then she would *also* be content going on a hike three or four days in a row. There were even times when she would not hike or get much exercise for a couple of weeks because I had gone on vacation and left her with my parents or a friend. It never seemed to make any difference to her.

One of the best things about hiking with a dog is that you never have to listen to complaints. It didn't matter what the conditions were or how long the hike was, Vaida just did it. Hiking was what we did. Once I stopped working my late-night schedule at Higher Ground and got a normal nine-to-five, Monday-to-Friday day job at Ibex, Saturdays and Sundays were our only hiking options. This meant I had to keep a close eye on the weather forecast at trailhead level and especially on the high peaks, because weather at four thousand feet could be very different. Fortunately, by this time I had a lot of hiking experience and knew which websites to use to get the information I needed regarding weather and trail conditions. If it was going to be an absolutely beautiful day, I would pick a hike where we would be hiking above-tree-line. If the forecast was calling for poor weather, rain or snow, I'd choose a trail that would be more tree covered.

Once I started having only my weekends to hike, I almost never let the weather deter me unless it would be dangerous to do so. I felt like I had enough hiking knowledge to avoid potential problems for us both. I also trusted that Vaida would be okay regardless of the weather. I always reasoned that she would be okay in any weather that I could tolerate. In fact, she could probably withstand colder weather than me. She had a big fur coat, after all. I always marveled at how she could be up on a mountain in zero-degree temperatures and blowing snow with an ice beard and she was fine. In fact, not only was she fine, she never changed her normal "I'm at the peak" routine. She would sit or lie down when we got to the top of the mountain, even in near whiteout conditions with the wind blowing forty miles per hour, and take it all in. Sometimes she would even take a nap in the middle of a snowstorm. At the height of her hiking, we hiked every single weekend the entire year.

vaida's adoption photo captured my heart the
moment i saw her beautiful bright eyes.

vaida and maggie waiting patiently outside
for their treat from the fedex guy.

enjoying a break from the 9-5 office grind, accompanying
me on a photo shoot in burlington, VT.

making her way across franconia ridge on a cold winter day.

taking a moment to marvel in her surroundings on glen boulder trail.

pausing for a photo as we head to the summit of mount moosilauke, our favorite NH 4000 foot mountain, which vaida climbed in every month throughout her hiking career.

patiently waiting outside the dungeon of lakes of
the clouds hut in whiteout conditions.

leading the way across the precarious jefferson snowfield.

may 22, 2016 – caitlin and vaida finish the NH48 on mount madison.

july 3, 2017 - vaida finishes the new england "doggie 64" on saddleback mountain in maine.

those beautiful bright eyes that looked deep into your heart and stole it, though i'm pretty sure she was staring at my lunch.

on june 30, 2022 i left vaida's ashes on saddleback mountain
in maine in memory of her completion of the "doggie 64".

at sunset on april 6, 2022 – i placed vaida's ashes near
the summit sign on mount moosilauke. the sun cast a ray
of light directly on the spot, a sign from vaida....

7

Vermont's Long Trail and the Unplanned Quest for the NH48

Constructed between 1910 and 1930, Vermont's Long Trail is the oldest long-distance trail in the country at 273 miles long, from Vermont's border with Massachusetts in the south to the Canadian border in the north. It runs through the state of Vermont, along the spine of the Green Mountains. Roughly one hundred miles of the trail coincide with the Appalachian Trail in the southern third of the state. At Maine Junction, which is near Killington, Vermont, the Long Trail continues north and the Appalachian Trail (A.T.) turns east toward New Hampshire and Maine. The Long Trail is a really popular first-time long-distance hike and a good way to figure out if you like backpacking and long-distance hiking.

The summer of 2015 while I was working at Ibex, I used two weeks of vacation time with the intention to hike the entire trail starting from the Massachusetts/Vermont border. This was going to be my first long-distance hike with Vaida.

During our first two days, we were able to cover a total of forty miles. Toward the end of our second day, my knee was beginning to bother me and I was ready to find a campsite. According to Guthook (the phone app generally used by hikers), there was a large campsite just north of the dirt road I was about to cross. I got to the road and found a large parking lot. Because I was such a newbie, I was having a hard time figuring out exactly what this meant. Did it mean I should walk up the road a ways, or did it mean continue north on the trail? I went with the first option, searching along the road, and I couldn't find the campsite. I walked a short way on the trail and still couldn't find it, so I decided to give up for the moment and head to the water source I had noticed earlier. Because I had to go down a short embankment to get to the water, I left Vaida resting in the parking lot with my pack. When I came back up, I saw a gal sitting on the other side of the parking lot and, sure enough, Vaida was sitting with her. I could see from afar that she had a very small pack and something about her told me she was an Appalachian Trail thru-hiker. I was really intimidated at the thought of approaching this clearly experienced hiker, but I had to get my dog. I learned her name was Tick Tock, and she was indeed hiking the A.T. She had started her hike in Georgia four months earlier. Having failed at finding the campsite, I hesitatingly and somewhat embarrassedly asked Tick Tock if she knew where it was. Of course, she did, so I asked if she minded camping with a dorky Long Trail hiker like me. We wound up having a really fun evening together, spending the night discussing gear and other long-distance trails she'd hiked and having silly girl talk over ramen, while Vaida snoozed nearby. I couldn't believe that this seasoned A.T. hiker wanted to hang out with me.

The following day, she invited us to hike along with her and the two friends she had been hiking with, Pork Chop and Lightning.

Very intimidated by the thought of hiking with A.T. hikers, I said, "You don't want this Long Trail rookie and her dog with you. You are veteran hikers, plus I'm not sure we'll be able to keep up."

Tick Tock insisted that we join, so Vaida and I spent the day hiking with her and met up with her friends later that evening. I really didn't think we would be able to keep up with them, but to my surprise, Vaida and I hiked three twenty-plus mile days with them, our biggest day being twenty-seven miles. This was our biggest day ever. I had set out with the ambitious goal of covering big miles each day while also seeing what Vaida was capable of, so I was very pleased with this.

Even though Vaida and I had just met these three hikers, we quickly hit it off. Sometimes Tick Tock and I would just stay back and chat while the guys hiked ahead. Since Vaida liked being at the front of the group, I had no problem letting her hike with them even when they got a good mile ahead of us. I never worried. Pork Chop really loved Vaida and watched out for her as if she were his own. I vividly recall one afternoon that still makes me smile. Pork Chop and Lightning were taking a break near a pond. When Tick Tock and I got there, Vaida was already in the water and Pork Chop happily told me not to worry, he had taken Vaida's backpack off before she went in because he figured I didn't want her getting it wet.

Unfortunately, with 160 miles still to cover, I only made it as far as Killington before I had to call it quits. Because it was my first long-distance hike, I didn't know much about proper foot care and my feet got beat up pretty badly. The Long Trail, especially the southern half, is notorious for being incredibly muddy and wet, hence the nickname used among many long-distance hikers, "Vermud." Even though I was wearing trail running shoes that dry quickly, I didn't give my feet time to dry out during the one long break I took each day and paid the price. By the time we got to Killington, my feet were killing me and I had developed a major blister problem. I had a horrible blister on the end of one of my toes. It was so big and so painful and unlike any blister I had ever seen before, so I started to lovingly refer to it as Dead Toe. I believe it developed from a combination of the moisture and stubbing it what seemed like hundreds of times on roots and rocks. On the pad of each foot, it seemed the first layer of skin had separated and moisture had gotten in between the layers. I'm not sure I would call it a blister, but whatever it was caused me so much pain I could barely walk. Vaida, on the other hand, was showing no signs or symptoms that the 110 miles she had covered over the course of five days was too much.

I had made a plan with the person I was dating at the time to drop off more food for me in Killington, but as soon as I saw his truck, I knew I needed to go home and stay off my feet for a few days. But first, I *had* to get rid of this blister. My new friends had a hotel room for the night and offered to let me shower, which gave me a chance to immediately tend to my feet. Poking a small needle in the blister on Dead Toe gave me some much needed relief. After everyone showered, we all headed to the local pub. While we all sat around happily stuffing our faces and laughing about the fun four days we'd had together, I was able to air out the pads of my feet. Vaida and I said goodbye to our new friends and looked forward to our return home and a whole lot more blister care while staying off my feet. It was really sad driving away from everyone and the trail.

The house I lived in at the time was right near the Appalachian Trail, and I knew Tick Tock, Pork Chop, and Lightning would be taking the next day off and then would be hiking eighteen miles to a road crossing right near my house. I sent Tick Tock a message and told her I'd be happy to pick them up and bring them back to my house for food and a comfy bed. They had enjoyed hiking with me and Vaida so much that during their stay with me, they tried hard to convince us to rejoin them on the Appalachian Trail. Even after two days of rest, I knew my feet were in no condition to keep up with their big miles, and I had a sneaking suspicion that there was no way we would even be able to complete the second half of the trail the following week. Tempting as their offer was, I said, "We can't. We are staying on the Long Trail." Then, I considered my options.

Hanging out with everyone at my house made me want to at least try and get back on the trail, so after saying what was to be our final goodbyes, I decided to get dropped off on the Long Trail twenty miles north of Killington to test out my feet and hike back south to Killington. Again, Vaida did great, but by the time I got to Killington, I was limping and could barely walk, never mind hike. My feet were so bad I ended up going to the doctor. The first person I saw was a physician's assistant. When he saw Dead Toe and the pads of my feet, it was if he had never seen anything like that before. He said, "What on earth did you do to them?" The only response I could come up with was, "Uh, hike?" Completely baffled, he had to call for backup so the doctor could instruct him on what to do. I don't remember exactly what he did, but whatever it was, as soon as he did it, I knew I was going to be losing the toenail. Beyond that, his only advice was to stay off my feet, so I decided to go to the beach for a week. This actually turned out to be a *really* bad idea because Dead Toe and the pads of my feet got completely filled with sand. What a disaster.

I was really disappointed. Were it not for my foot problems, I would have completed the Long Trail in one trip. Unlike me, Vaida did absolutely fine. That was her first time hiking big miles every day. In the end, she hiked 130 miles in six days, and she loved it. She was having the time of her life, meeting people, living in the woods, and at no point did

I have any concerns about her health or well-being. I was so proud of her, but I was really bummed with myself.

I knew I wanted to finish the Long Trail, so we wound up completing it in a handful of weekends during the rest of the summer and fall, backpacking on two- or three-day trips. It was kind of a pain because I had to figure out getting to a trailhead, leaving my car, and then getting back to it when I was done. Often, I was able to coordinate rides with friends, but sometimes I had to hitchhike. I wouldn't feel comfortable hitchhiking just anywhere, but hitchhiking in known "trail towns" has always felt safe to me. Most local folks are really generous and kind and know that when they see someone with an overnight backpack, they simply need a ride either to get more supplies, to find a bed for the night, or to get to another point on the trail. They also know they will probably have to roll the windows down to air out the hiker smell after, and don't seem to mind for the most part.

Meeting Tick Tock, Pork Chop, and Lightning on that first half of our Long Trail adventure really did a lot to boost my hiking confidence, and I think the whole hike would have been very different had I not met them. Had Vaida not found Tick Tock that night in the parking lot, I probably would have never met them. Here were these three very experienced A.T. hikers who had been on the trail for four months, with 1,700 miles under their belts, and we were able to easily keep up with them. I had plenty of experience taking Vaida on long day hikes, but I was a brand-new backpacker on my first overnight trip ever, and they wanted Vaida and me to hike with them. They didn't consider me a rookie backpacker and said that Vaida and I seemed to know what we were doing. That was really cool.

Having the right gear and a lot of determination to consistently do big miles helped too. Through a combination of my own research and the advice of someone I had met earlier that year, I learned how to pack super minimally and light while still having all of the essential gear to safely spend multiple nights in the woods. I had become "ultralight," a term commonly used in the backpacking world, meaning your total pack weight is under ten pounds before adding food and water. Even with food and water, my pack often only weighed fifteen pounds, and even less as I ate. This allowed me to move quickly and efficiently. Having Vaida carry her own supplies in a custom pack made by a small cottage company called Groundbird Gear also helped reduce the weight I was carrying.

While Vaida and I worked on completing the second half of the Long Trail during the fall and summer of 2015, we also resumed our routine day hiking in Vermont and slowly started to explore New Hampshire. I had always been opposed to hiking in New Hampshire because I was intimidated by the unfamiliar scenery and terrain. Knowing how passionate I was about hiking, friends would often encourage me to go to New Hampshire and explore the White Mountains, but my stubborn response was always, "I live in Vermont. I want to hike in Vermont and see Vermont things. Why would I go to New Hampshire?"

In spite of my love affair with Vermont, earlier that year in March, Vaida and I were introduced to the White Mountains and I realized there might be more out there worth exploring. Michael, an Ibex coworker and experienced hiker, knew that Vaida and I spent every weekend hiking in Vermont but had never been to New Hampshire. One winter weekend, he and two other Ibex coworkers, Squirrel and Sarah, planned to hike Mount Moosilauke and invited us along. I think he had secretly been waiting for this opportunity for months. He knew the beauty that the White Mountains held and that once Vaida and I got a taste of it, we'd want to keep coming back for more. He was right.

We strapped snowshoes to the tops of our packs on that cold, overcast March day and hiked to the summit of the 4,802-foot mountain. I remember being a little intimidated, not only because it stood at almost five thousand feet but it was winter and it was a hike Vaida and I had never done. But based on all of our other adventures and miles covered in Vermont, I knew we could do it. I have very vivid memories of Vaida just ambling along through the snow like it was any old hike. The mountain that day had no views and was completely socked in by the clouds, but when we reached the summit and I saw Vaida lying in the snow, the feeling that I got was bigger than any other feeling I had had hiking thus far. We may as well have climbed Everest that day. I couldn't believe what we had been missing out on.

Vaida and I had spent plenty of time above four thousand feet in Vermont, hiking Camel's Hump and Mount Mansfield regularly during the spring, summer, and fall and here we were on top of another beautiful four-thousand-foot mountain in the winter in our neighboring state only a short drive away. The following week at work, I couldn't stop thinking about that hike or talking about it. I was literally on cloud nine. I was really sore too.

As I reflect on Vaida's and my experiences and progression as hikers, I realize that it wasn't until this snowy hike with my Ibex coworkers nearly six years into Vaida's life that we had truly developed as avid year-round hikers. Up until this point, I had essentially thought that, once you saw the first dusting of snow on the high peaks in Vermont, it meant time to hang up your hiking boots, and Vaida and I had found other ways to exercise and enjoy the snow from lower elevations. Hiking with my coworkers with snowshoes strapped to our packs and making it to the snowy mountain top gave me the confidence that this was something Vaida and I should keep doing.

At the time, I wasn't aware of the New Hampshire 48. I only knew I had just been on this incredible hike and wanted to see more. A few weeks later, Vaida and I hiked Mount Moosilauke again and started to look for more opportunities to explore the White Mountains. Because it was all so unfamiliar, I was a little hesitant to venture into this vast wilderness alone. In May of that year, Vaida and I went on a three-day backpacking trip to hike Mount Moosilauke and South and North Kinsman with my friend Jason who I had met through the Appalachian Trail social media network. He was hiking the entire A.T., and Vaida and I agreed to hike as long or as far as he had planned for those three days. That experience was a huge confidence boost for me because we were able to do fifteen- to twenty-mile days in the White Mountains, which is some of the hardest, most rugged terrain on the Appalachian Trail. It was reassuring knowing that Vaida could handle it as well.

Having started to explore New Hampshire, one day at work my friend Michael asked me if I was planning on hiking the 48. *The 48?* I didn't know what that was. He explained to me that there are forty-eight mountains in New Hampshire that are over four thousand feet and that people make it a goal to hike all of them. I couldn't believe there were that many four-thousand-foot mountains close to where I lived.

Vermont has five four-thousand-foot mountains that are beautiful, but the landscape and scenery in New Hampshire, particularly above-tree-line and on the mountain peaks, was unlike anything I had ever seen before. A few days later, Michael brought me a set of trail maps and the White Mountain Guide with the list, description, and trip planning advice for each of the four-thousand-footers and hikes throughout the Whites.

Although I never was typically a "list" person, I decided to print a list of the New Hampshire 48 in order to keep track of what Vaida and I were very slowly starting to chip away at. I had no intention of completing them in any sort of set time frame. Every time I hiked one for the first time, I'd write in the date and who I did it with (usually just Vaida) and hang it at my desk. Even though I knew there were at least forty-eight different possibilities each weekend, I still wouldn't do a new peak every weekend. I had my favorites, so I kept hiking the ones I knew and enjoyed. Every time it was nice out, or I just felt like it, I went to Moosilauke or Franconia Ridge, because they had some of the best views and were so beautiful.

In order to plan my weekend hikes, I was constantly checking the weather for the White Mountains. By the time Friday rolled around, if I saw that the forecast was calling for crummy weather, I would ask Michael for his advice on what peak to hike. For these days, we would choose a hike that was below tree line and without the great views. Even though some of the hikes were boring and viewless, there was still something special about experiencing each one for the first time and being able to check them off the list.

In April 2016, Michael, who would ask me every Monday what Vaida and I did that weekend, rolled his eyes when he heard we had repeated yet another one of our favorite hikes. He asked to see my list and pointed out that I only had a few left (most of them were the long, boring ones typically left to the end by hikers hoping to complete the NH48). Michael went on to say I could probably do the 48 within a year if I stopped repeating the same hikes over and over again. Since Memorial Day of 2015, Vaida and I had completed thirty-six of the 48, leaving us with just twelve peaks to go. Sometimes you can link multiple summits together, so it wasn't going to be twelve separate hikes.

I told him I wasn't trying to do them all in a year, was just enjoying myself and my time spent with Vaida. He pointed out that if we did the remaining twelve peaks, we would finish all forty-eight within a year's time and that would be pretty cool to be able to say.

That really lit a fire under me. Although I was never really into tracking my accomplishments, completing the 48 was something I at least wanted to do in my lifetime. Realizing this was something Vaida and

I could accomplish together was really motivating. It would also mean that I could be *done*, Michael would stop bugging me, and we could continue to hike Mount Moosilauke and Franconia Ridge to our heart's content. The next handful of weekends, I was dead set on us getting them done by Memorial Day weekend. Even though it would only take a few weekends to do, the spring hiking conditions in the White Mountains were not always ideal due to the unpredictable weather, snowmelt, and refreeze making it a little more difficult. Nonetheless, it was a challenge I was willing to give myself and Vaida.

A lot of people, when they complete the NH48, have a big celebration. They get a bunch of their hiking friends together and all hike up the final peak together. I was going to finish with just one friend. It was just Vaida and me. I look back now and realize how big of a deal it was. It seemed so routine to me, but it wasn't. It took a lot of time, motivation, dedication, gas money, and driving. These peaks are all above four thousand feet. You do a lot of hiking above-tree-line, sometimes in rough conditions. Seven of the 48 are above five thousand feet in elevation, including Mount Washington, which is 6,288 feet. It's not easy. But Vaida and I did it.

A few things happened once I set my mind to completing the 48 within a year. The main thing was that I discovered the existence of a huge hiking community consisting of a myriad of like-minded, outdoor loving hiking enthusiasts like me. People would come from all over to work on completing their list. Hiking in Vermont, where I had spent most of my early hiking days, was very different. There were only five four-thousand-foot mountains, and it seemed to me it was mostly just folks out for a fun hike on a beautiful day, nodding a quick hello as we crossed paths. But when you're in New Hampshire, especially if you were on one of the less popular trails, when you crossed paths with someone, they would almost always stop you and say, "Are you working on the 48?" It was so cool to converse with a fellow hiker about all of the mountains and different trails and their experiences. More often than not, the sight of Vaida and her calm demeanor and beautiful appearance created the perfect icebreaker for me to start talking with a complete stranger. As I continued to hike the 48, this seemed to repeatedly happen. I can say without a doubt that I have Vaida to thank for helping me break out of my shell and become the outgoing, talkative person I am today.

When Vaida and I were working on completing the 48 during those last six weeks, cramming the hikes in to make sure we finished, we saw a lot of the same people. One day, Vaida and I were doing a traverse between Mount Waumbek and Mount Cabot and spent the night camped at the cabin on Cabot. Coming down the mountain in the morning, I ran into a girl named Courtney who was on the way up. She was hiking with her father, and she stopped me and said, "Hey, we saw you guys on Isolation the other week. I remember your dog." This was when I started to realize that Vaida and I were becoming a recognizable hiking duo. Sure, it hurt my feelings a little that really it was Vaida she recognized, but how could such a big, beautiful dog not stand out?

Earlier that year, Vaida and I met a girl named Christine when we were doing a winter hike on Franconia Ridge. I started talking to her because she was wearing an Ibex hat. To my surprise, she told me that her cousin worked with me at Ibex. A couple of weeks later, Vaida and I were staying at a hostel we had started frequenting and ran into Christine again. She said, "You work at Ibex with my cousin. I met you guys on Franconia Ridge." She and I quickly became friends, exchanged numbers, and made plans to go on a hike together. Again, surely Vaida was who she really recognized, but this was when I started to realize that the White Mountains hiking community just may be a little smaller and more close-knit than I had previously thought.

A couple of months after we finished the 48, Christine called and asked me if I wanted to go for a hike. Vaida and I had just done a thirty-six-mile overnight hike in Maine called the Grafton Loop. Because it had been a hot and difficult hike, I promised Vaida that we could take the next day off and go swimming. But when Christine called me and said, "I'm going to hike the Wildcats tomorrow, do you and Vaida want to come?" I couldn't resist.

While we were hiking, she told me about this really nice girl she had met named Courtney who was working on the 48. This was just a random conversation while hiking. Not long after that conversation, we were standing under the chairlift on the top of Wildcat Mountain, taking a break and taking in the views of Mount Washington, when we saw a group of hikers walking toward us. Christine immediately recognized one of them. It was Courtney! The very same girl she had just been telling me about. What was even stranger, was when Courtney looked at me and Vaida she said, "We saw you guys going up Cabot! We were the ones who said we had seen you on Isolation." It was unbelievable how connected everyone who is working on the 48 can be. Christine and Courtney are just two examples of the great friends I have made through hiking. Before I adopted Vaida, I kept to myself a lot more. Were it not for Vaida, I'm not sure they would have remembered me.

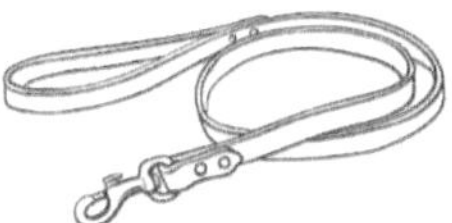

After completing the New Hampshire 48, I figured we might as well do "the New England 67," which consists of all of the mountains over four thousand feet in New England. I had already done the 48 in New Hampshire and the five peaks in Vermont, with the remaining fourteen peaks being in Maine. The one asterisk to this would be that Vaida wasn't allowed on three of the fourteen four-thousand-footers in Maine (Katahdin, Hamlin, and North Brother). These peaks are in Baxter State Park, and the park doesn't allow dogs. I started calling what Vaida could do the "Doggie 64."

Just like the 48, I realized it was a tangible goal for Vaida and me to accomplish. I didn't care about being able to say that *I* hiked the NE67, but to say Vaida did, now that was cool! Given that all but one (Old Speck) of the fourteen Maine peaks were far away, the logistics to hike these would take some planning, so I wasn't in any real rush. So for now, Vaida and I continued doing some of our favorite hikes on the list of the 48 in New Hampshire over and over and over again.

It had been two years since that first overnight backpacking adventure on the Long Trail when we met Tick Tock, so my skill and knowledge had drastically increased by this point. I had been lucky enough to begin backpacking as an "ultralight" hiker, and it seemed my pack was only getting lighter as I shed any nonessential items and continued to research the best and lightest-weight gear available. Vaida and I had covered hundreds of miles backpacking in those past two years, and I had learned how to carry everything I needed and nothing that I didn't. It certainly helped that, in these experiences, we met countless other knowledgeable hikers and I was learning more and more tricks on how to shed weight. This meant we could move faster and cover miles more easily along the trail. My favorite way to hike when on overnight trips became hiking from sunup until sundown.

After completing the 48 in May of 2016, Vaida and I spent the next few months strictly hiking in the White Mountains. When I saw that I had a long Fourth of July weekend, I decided we should take this experience we had gained over the years and go explore Maine for the first time. I knew it would be no problem to hike the first of the eleven peaks in Maine, Old Speck, on a thirty-six-mile overnight trip on the Grafton Loop. That would leave ten.

On the long Fourth of July weekend the following year, 2017, Jodeob and I decided it was a perfect weekend to finish Vaida's "Doggie 64." I had done some research on the best way to knock out these ten, and it appeared we could hike eight of them by doing a thirty-two-mile stretch of trail on the Appalachian Trail between Stratton and Rangeley and the other two in a day hike. Our first day in Maine, we hiked two of them, Bigelow Avery and Bigelow West Peak, and the following day we left to do the thirty-two-mile overnight hike from Stratton to Rangeley.

Of course, to make it more difficult on us, some of those peaks aren't directly on the A.T. and, for a handful of them, we would have to take side trails off the A.T., making it a forty-two-mile overnight trip. Most of the side trails were well-marked trails, but one of them is what's referred to as "a bushwhack." It's essentially a "herd path." Everyone knows about the bushwhack out to Mount Redington, but it is not a maintained trail, it is not marked. I will never forget that side trail adventure. We made it out to Mount Redington with no problem, but for some reason we got really confused trying to retrace our steps on the bushwhack back to the Appalachian Trail. This area was right near where a woman had disappeared a few years earlier and they never found her body until several years later. We had just been talking about that, and here we were lost in the exact area, in the really dense, thick Maine woods. It was really nerve-racking.

For over an hour, we wandered around not able to find the Appalachian Trail. We just kept walking farther away from where we had come from. The trees had gotten thicker, and we were surrounded by dense woods, but we were on this weird old wide trail. For some reason it reminded me of an old ski trail, and there were also a lot of logging roads that crossed over it. Luckily, we had our A.T. Guthook app on our phones and used it to show us our location. We realized we were too far away and would have to walk through the dense woods to get back to the A.T. where we had originally left it. We figured out if we kept going down the old wide trail, we would junction with a river and could walk along the river back to the A.T. Meanwhile, Vaida continued to amble along with us as if we were just out on a regular hike.

Things didn't get any better once we made it to the river, because our next obstacle was a very angry beaver. The river was raging from a torrential downpour the night before, and I think the beaver probably lost his home and was very upset. I was worried that he was going to attack Vaida. Despite this being our first run-in with an angry animal while hiking, Vaida didn't even pay attention to him. The beaver was about twenty feet away from us and kept hissing at us and standing up on his hind legs, so Jodeob wound up throwing rocks in his direction to try to scare him off. We didn't know what to do, and there was no way to go around him. We really did think he was going to attack us. He finally gave up the fight and decided to waddle away in the same direction we were walking. We had to walk very slowly behind him until we eventually reached the Appalachian Trail. Jodeob and I were so relieved to finally be back on track, but things didn't end there, because we were right at a point where the trail crossed the wide, raging river. The same river that probably knocked out the angry beaver's home. It seemed like a pretty difficult and precarious crossing, but there was a board we could use for part of the crossing, and it was the only safe place to get across the river.

The same time that we started our crossing, a hiker with a large dog on the other side of the river started across. Jodeob went first with Vaida to make sure she made it safely, but for some reason, as they were walking across the board, Vaida fell in. Thank goodness she had her harness on because she was getting pulled by the river under the board. Jodeob was able to grab her by the harness and hold onto her. If he hadn't grabbed her, she would have gotten swept away. This was the scariest situation I had ever been in with Vaida while we were hiking.

The hiker with the dog was able to help us get her out of the water while I stood back with my heart beating a thousand miles an hour. It was absolutely gut-wrenching. Between getting lost on the bushwhack, the angry beaver, and the river crossing, it was a really intense portion of the trip. And it wasn't done yet. We still had two four-thousand-footers to get over and thirteen miles left to Rangeley. After the crossing, things calmed down for us and we wound up making it up to the Horn and the Saddlebacks, Vaida's final peaks, right as the sun was setting. We were the only people up there, and it was the most stunning way to finish Vaida's Doggie 64. A beautiful night above the tree line, in an open alpine zone, watching the sunset. I took a moment to look back at all of the adventures, all of the miles we had covered, and the difficulty of some of those hikes we had been on in order to achieve this feat, and I started to cry. I will never forget that night. As I reflected on all that we had accomplished, Vaida did what she always did on the top of a mountain. She took a nap.

People know that I am driven and what I am capable of. Doing those ten summits in Maine's rough terrain in one long weekend was fairly ambitious, especially with a big dog, but I was confident in Vaida. Everyone knew about Vaida and that she was capable of backpacking, camping, and hiking twenty to twenty-five miles a day. It wasn't a new thing for her. She had already logged hundreds of miles in that manner.

In June 2022, a few months after Vaida died, I hiked the final three peaks in Baxter State Park in order to complete the New England 67. I carried her ashes with me on each of those three peaks, so in a sense, she summitted all sixty-seven with me.

8

The Hiking Community

The hiking community is one of the main reasons I still enjoy hiking so much. Certainly, the scenery and the exercise have always been a large part of it, but the people I've met and the lasting friendships I've formed are the main reasons I keep going back. Whether it is an incredibly accomplished hiking couple always there to lend me advice, a well-known hiker willing to hang out with a lesser known hiker like me, a family of eight teaching me lessons about life and responsibility, or simply the random people I run into throughout my hiking adventures, I can't think of a better group of people to spend my time with. And while Vaida may not have been directly responsible for my meeting all of these amazing individuals, I can say with certainty that the reason my hiking community has become like family to me was because of my relationship with her and her magical ability to break down my shy shell and expose my talkative and outgoing personality.

My work environments were smaller, more like a petri dish of the same forty or so like-minded people, day in and day out, where even the shyest person would eventually talk to others and make friends. When I was out hiking, I would see a different forty people on the trail every day because the hiking community is more like a revolving door of forty million people, all with different stories and personalities and backgrounds.

So many people with a lot more experience and knowledge than me, and when I really immersed myself in that world, I felt like a complete newbie and often even more nervous about talking to new people. Vaida helped me through that, helped me grow to become part of that community, like she was the catalyst for what could be likened to immersion therapy for my introverted personality.

One of the unique things about this community are the trail names many hikers get. Some are obvious, like "Mr. Sunshine," who often wore a bright shirt and was always happy and upbeat. A couple that I met while they were on their honeymoon, Hannah and Daniel, probably got their nicknames of "Salt and Pepper" because they seemed like the perfect pair. "Cucumber" got his name because somebody dropped his camera off a cliff and he was "cool as a cucumber" about it. Hikers give other hikers their trail names, and these names often reflect something funny that happened or something funny that they did.

I don't have a trail name that's stuck. Cucumber called me "Beam" because I drove a BMW and because he said that I had a smile that beamed and "lit up the room." Mr. Sunshine liked to call me "Chips" because one time, when we were lying in the tent with Vaida directly outside the open door, a chipmunk leaped over Vaida, came running in, hit me in the head, and ran back out. I also always carried potato chips as a trail snack and have a teddy bear named Chips. Everyone else just calls me Caitlin.

Having always done the majority of our hiking as just Vaida and me, it wasn't until the fall of 2015 that we were introduced to the hiking community. Once we caught the NH48 bug, Vaida and I found ourselves venturing over to the White Mountains a few weekends a month. Wanting to hike both Saturday and Sunday, we would stay in a dog-friendly motel room Saturday night. The memories and four-thousand-footers checked off the list started to build, but so did the expense.

Looking online for a cheaper way to spend the weekend, I stumbled upon The Notch Hostel located in North Woodstock, New Hampshire in the heart of the White Mountains. The Notch is a four-thousand-square-foot 1890s farmhouse converted into a thirty-guest hostel by owners Serena Ryan and Justin Walsh. Within the walls of the beautiful farmhouse, you find a boot room to dry your gear, a large communal kitchen, and a living room with a warm fireplace, four bunk rooms, and two private rooms. Outside there is a large porch to gather on, three decks, a gear shed for A.T. thru-hikers, tent sites, picnic tables, and a fire pit. As the hostel has grown over the years, it seems they are always finding creative ways to house more and more happy hikers.

I had stayed in hostels while traveling overseas during my college years. I went to South Africa to visit a friend who was studying abroad, and we spent a week in a rental car, traveling the country and staying in hostels. Shortly after graduating from college, my folks and I went to visit my brother who was studying abroad in Copenhagen, Denmark. Part of our trip to Denmark included a few days' stop in Iceland. The hostels there, however, were very upscale. I really had no idea what to expect, having never stayed in a hostel in the US and certainly never with Vaida.

I remember being a little hesitant to click the "book" button, and never in a million years did I think this one click would initiate the start of a lifetime of friendship filled with amazing memories and adventure and would form the foundation for my and Vaida's new basecamp. The Notch became our second home, our home away from home. The Notch isn't just a place to lay your head after a long hike. It's a place to commune and gather. A place to chat with other hikers and discuss plans for the next day or tell stories of that day's adventure. It's a place where you will meet people two to three times your age. A place where you'll meet skiers, bikers, and travelers, each with their own story to share with others. A place where you will make friends and gain instant community.

That first night Vaida and I stayed there, we were brightly greeted by Justin and welcomed with open arms. We instantly felt like we were at home, and I immediately felt comfortable letting Vaida do her typical Vaida thing. I felt comfortable leaving her off leash, letting her find a place to snooze on her own, leaving her alone while I milled about the hostel, chatting with other guests. More often than not, when I would return, I'd find Justin or a guest sitting on the floor with her, petting her.

After that first unforgettable stay, Vaida and I started coming back to The Notch at least once a month, and before I knew it, Serena and I were hiking together and forming a friendship that will last an eternity. Soon Vaida and I were regulars, returning every Friday night as soon as we got off work at Ibex and staying the entire weekend and waking up early on Monday to return to work. Luckily, it was only a little over an hour's drive. Definitely not a bad commute for a weekend's worth of adventure!

Of course, the goal each weekend was to hike, but it also soon became about being as immersed in the hiking community as possible. I loved returning to the hostel after a long day's hike and being able to leave Vaida wherever she felt comfortable while I did my shower and food routine. I was the one who had to do the talking, but I let Vaida be the one to draw people in. People would say, "Whose dog is this?" Someone else would say, "That's Caitlin's. She's here all the time. Vaida is a wonderful dog." Then people would meet me and say, "Oh my gosh, your dog, what an angel." We would talk about where we had hiked that day or pull out a map and chat about options for the next day's adventure. Over the course of a year, Vaida and I spent so much time at The Notch and made so many friendships and connections with regulars and staff and the close-knit community within the four farmhouse walls that we became a part of what Serena and I dubbed "The Hamily." Hostel Family.

The Hamily formed in the summer of 2016. I had taken one week off from work and was planning to attempt a "direttissima," which is when you connect all forty-eight four-thousand-footers into one continuous footpath over the course of approximately 250 miles. It requires carrying all of the food and supplies you need to spend each night in the woods until you've hiked all forty-eight four-thousand-footers. Not even twenty-four hours into what was expected to be a nine-day trip, my plans drastically changed. But that's okay, because what happened instead was even better.

I was spending the night at The Notch before starting the direttissima the next day, when I met this really nice gentleman nicknamed Cucumber. He was hiking the Appalachian Trail southbound from Maine to Georgia with his daughter, Sydney, whose trail name was Hummingbird. While this was her trail name, for some reason I chose to always refer to her by her first name. Part of my introduction to Cucumber and Sydney was learning that her younger brother, Joey, had just come to New Hampshire from Michigan where they lived. He was sixteen or seventeen years old and a typical teenage kid doing things that typical teenagers do. He wasn't planning on doing any hiking with his father and sister. He was planning on having a fun summer with his friends. One day, out of the blue, his mom put him in the car and didn't tell him where they were going. They drove from Michigan to New Hampshire, and she told him he was going to be hiking with his sister and dad for the next few weeks.

Joey seemed pretty upset about that change in plans. I just thought that was so funny. The father and daughter set out to hike this 2200-mile trail, and Joey was thinking he was going to have this grand old summer back home but instead ended up getting dragged to the Appalachian Trail.

They went on to tell me that the section of the trail where Joey started his hike with his dad and sister was the Carters and Wildcats, which I knew was one of the hardest sections of the White Mountains and thought to myself, *Man, what a section for that boy to have to start his hike on.* The next section of trail they had to tackle was the Presidential Range, and this was where they met another Appalachian Trail southbound hiker who was also staying at the hostel, Mr. Sunshine. He was this incredibly energetic, magnetic and funny guy. The fact that he was wearing a brightly colored T-shirt probably helped him earn the nickname. But really it was because he had this aura about him. He was excited all the time. He loved everything. He was just a very happy, energetic, outgoing person.

Cucumber and I hit it off and instantly became friends. I don't even know why we started chatting, but it was probably because of Vaida. I really enjoyed being around him and watching him interact with his kids as well as with Mr. Sunshine. There was an interesting and amusing dynamic between all four of them. As it turned out, Sydney needed to go home to Michigan for a week. She had recently graduated from college and needed to go home to work on her portfolio and website in order to receive an award in textile design. That left Cucumber and Joey stuck at the hostel for a week while Sydney was gone. A change in plans you could tell Joey definitely was not disappointed about. Instead of hiking, he got to hang out at the hostel with the revolving door of guests from all walks of life.

While standing around the firepit that night, I told Cucumber, "Vaida and I are about to attempt this really difficult hike and be gone in the woods for a week. You guys are stuck here. Take my car keys. Use my car. You seem nice. I trust you. All you have to do is bring Vaida and me to the start of the trail tomorrow." I don't know why I did that. I just trusted him. Plus, I was slowly learning that's what hikers do, they take care of one another.

So the next day, Cucumber drove Vaida and me to Mount Moosilauke to start the direttissima. We had gotten a late start because it was raining hard that morning, but we waited it out and it turned out to be a beautiful day. Under bright, sunny skies, Vaida and I said goodbye to Cucumber, leaving him with the keys to my ten-year-old BMW, and we went up and over Moosilauke and came down to a parking lot in Kinsmen Notch. There were a bunch of lawn chairs and people handing out burgers and dogs and beer and soda and potato chips to hungry hikers on the Appalachian Trail and invited us over. How exciting, trail magic on our first day!

I found myself sitting in a chair and thinking, *What the hell am I doing?! Here I am, hanging out with these nice people and other hikers. Why would I try to do this incredibly hard hike in nine days? I'm supposed to be on vacation.* I kind of knew right then and there that I wasn't going to complete the direttissima. In order to successfully complete the trip in just over one week, I was going to have to be fast and efficient. There was no way I was turning down a lawn chair, snack, and a cold drink. I wound up sitting in that parking lot for more than an hour, relaxing, chatting with people, and realizing Vaida and I weren't going to complete this crazy project. Even still, we finally said goodbye and continued on the path, setting up camp and heading toward the next mountains we'd need to conquer South and North Kinsman. We woke up the next morning, and while we were still doing what we had set out to do, I knew that we weren't going to finish it.

After breaking down camp in the morning, we hiked over the Kinsmans, and when we got to the top of Cannon Mountain, the route plan was to hike down a certain trail and walk along a bike path before setting up camp for the night. While standing on the top of Cannon, Vaida and I met some folks, we got chatting, and I explained to them what we were attempting but also that we were kind of "over it." They were so kind and told me that if we hiked down with them, they could give us a ride somewhere. One of the rules of the direttissima is to not accept rides or help from strangers, but I knew a good place to camp near the trail. Franconia Ridge was my next goal, so I had them drop me off in the parking lot and the true trip was officially aborted. Well, that's not true. It was already aborted when I'd accepted the trail magic. Tired and hungry, I wanted to text Cucumber and ask him to bring me some pizza, but I didn't have any cell phone service. So Vaida and I set up our camp, ate dinner, and went to sleep.

The next morning, I packed up and we went on to Franconia Ridge. I had learned that there was rainy weather coming in the next few days, so I took it as the perfect opportunity to leave the woods and head back to The Notch. Serena was excited when I called her for a ride because she was taking Cucumber and Mr. Sunshine to a concert that night and now I could join them. Reflecting on that fun concert evening, I don't remember what I did with Vaida for the night. I imagine I just left her snoozing away with one of the many hostel staff members or guests who also loved her.

As I was falling asleep in the comfy hostel bed that night, I said to myself, *That was a fun hiking adventure. I think Vaida and I will just hang out here for the next few days and go on some day hikes.*

And that's what we did. We hiked and hung out with Cucumber and Joey, who seemed to be enjoying his summer a bit more by this time, I'm guessing largely because while he wasn't with his friends back in Michigan, he also currently wasn't hiking with his dad and sister. We went antique shopping, out to restaurants, bought their food resupply, hung out by the fire, laughed a lot, and simply enjoyed meeting all of the other hikers at the hostel. Mr. Sunshine had left for a night to cover a sixteen-mile section of the trail with the intention of coming back to the hostel before continuing his southbound A.T. hike. He loved it there. He got to do things like build a pergola and a firepit. He also helped Serena with hostel chores in exchange for some free nights. I'm pretty sure, all told, he spent an entire week there. His work ethic and glowing personality really impressed me, and his presence was definitely missed by all while he was gone for two days.

There was also this really nice couple staying there who were new to the A.T., Hannah (Salt) and her husband, Daniel (Pepper). They were from Kansas and the sweetest people ever, and they absolutely adored Vaida. They were having a hell of a time through Maine and New Hampshire. It was their first backpacking trip and their honeymoon. I remember them telling us about all of the stuff that they carried to start. They showed me and Mr. Sunshine a picture of the gear they started with, and it was enough gear for four hikers! We all enjoyed a chuckle as they said, "We didn't know what we were doing." They ended up having to stash some of their stuff in the Maine hundred-mile wilderness. Daniel got the GPS coordinates, and when they got out of the hundred-mile wilderness, they had family drive them back into the wilderness to find all of the camping gear they'd ditched because it was just too heavy for them. They made it another 270 miles to the hostel to tell their story and were taking a few rest days. Daniel was really handy, so he helped out with fixing a lawnmower and building and painting various things throughout the hostel grounds. It was an interesting group of people, the father and son, exuberant Mr. Sunshine, this really lovely couple, and a girl and her dog, all meeting at random. We all just really clicked.

One afternoon, Justin said to me, "Caitlin, this is the best group of hikers we've had all year, hands down. Maybe that we've *ever* had. I want to throw a barbecue for them because Sydney is going to be back tonight and they're all getting back on trail tomorrow." And that's just what Justin did. He threw a big outdoor party. That night we were all hanging out, eating by the fire, when I turned to Cucumber, Sydney, and Mr. Sunshine and said, "Today is only Thursday. I still have three days of vacation left. Why don't I just get on the trail with you guys? We can all walk south and then on Sunday I'll figure out how to get back to my car with Vaida. No big deal. That will be fun." I was guessing they'd be covering approximately fifty miles during those three days, so it really did sound fun and I wasn't worried at all about finding a way back to my car.

The next afternoon, we got dropped off at the base of Moosilauke and started walking on the A.T. as a group of hikers. It was Cucumber, Sydney, Joey, Mr. Sunshine, Vaida, and me. I didn't care where we ended up on the third day, because I was confident it would be somewhere close to where I lived and worked and if hitching back to the hostel failed, I could always call a coworker for help. When we were leaving, one of the hostel staff who we really hit it off with, named Kale, said to me, "If you get really jammed up and need a ride back to your car, call me." Now I had another option. We left without a care in the world, not thinking about my car and how far away I was going to be from it.

Mr. Sunshine, Vaida, and I ended up hiking ahead of the others as we descended Mount Moosilauke. As we hiked down the mountain, he said he was going to do what he called a "hero run." I didn't know what that meant, so he explained that he knew the shelter we planned to stay at was less than two miles from a road. He was going to drop all of his stuff at the shelter, hike down to the road, and then hitchhike to the store and get everyone a bunch of beers. This sounded like a fun adventure that I wanted to be a part of, but I had Vaida with me. Luckily, when we got down to the shelter, there was an A.T. north-bounder hiking from Georgia to Maine already there, so I looked at him and said, "Hey, will you watch my dog? Oh, and do you want anything from the store?"

Because it was an odd request, he looked at me like I was a little crazy, but then said, "Sure, I don't mind." I gave Vaida a kiss on the head, told her that I would think about her the entire time I was gone, and left her with this random A.T. hiker while Mr. Sunshine and I ran down the trail. As soon as we got to the road, we met an older gentleman sitting by the trail who said he'd give us a ride to the gas station. We bought a couple twelve-packs of beer, soda for Joey, and a bag of ice, put it in Mr. Sunshine's backpack, and hitchhiked back to the trail feeling like heroes. When we discovered two of the cans of beer had burst in Mr. Sunshine's backpack on our run back, we felt a little less heroic. Two lost beers and a backpack that was going to smell like stale beer and hiker funk for the next few days, if not weeks, was just gross.

I had so much fun that night hanging out with my new friends. I think Joey had a great time too because he got to spend time with a bunch of crazy hikers and see all of the wild and crazy things they do. He was slowly acclimating to the trail and liking it a little bit more. Plus, Mr. Sunshine made everything so much fun.

While we were on that trip, something clicked between me and Mr. Sunshine. We were having so much fun together and really hitting it off conversationally. Our connection really developed when we were on a mountain in southern New Hampshire called Mount Cube. For days I had been talking to the gang about the side trail out to North Peak. I had been telling them that from the South Peak all you could see was Vermont and the mountains like Killington ahead on the A.T., but if you took the side trail to North Peak, you could look back at everything you had just hiked over. We were ahead of Cucumber, Sydney, and Joey, so I took Mr. Sunshine on the side trail to check it out while we waited for them to catch up. It was when we were sitting there taking in the view of Mount Moosilauke that we realized we liked each other. This was after hanging out on the trail for twenty-four hours and a little bit at the hostel during the week. There was something about his energetic, magnetic personality and his work ethic that I was really attracted to. But what stood out the most was the attention and care he showed Vaida. He had just met her, yet he was treating her as if she were his own.

By the end of the next day, he said, "I'm coming with you to get your car."

I reminded him that he was on the Appalachian Trail.

He said, "I don't care. I'm coming with you to get your car. We'll camp at the hostel, and in the morning, you can drive me back to the trail before you go to work." We ended up close to Hanover, New Hampshire on Sunday afternoon, near where I worked, so that was fine, but we still had to figure out how to get back to my car at The Notch Hostel. I remembered what Kale had said about helping me out and when I called, he said it would be no problem. Kale was there to get us in less than an hour, and we were back at The Notch in no time. Kale is now one of my best friends.

This impromptu three-day hike worked out perfectly. The only downside was saying goodbye to my new friends, Cucumber, Sydney, and Joey, but I somehow knew that I would be seeing them again. In the morning, I dropped Mr. Sunshine off at the trail exactly where we had stopped the night before and went to work at Ibex. He hiked that Monday, and Vaida and I met him and the rest of the gang after work and we camped in the woods. I woke up and went to work the next day, and Mr. Sunshine decided to take the day off and stayed in town at what is called a "trail angel's" house, people who let hikers stay at their house for free. After work, I met up with him, and Vaida and I stayed at the trail angel's house with him. Despite all of the shuffling around, Vaida didn't seem to have a care in the world as long as she had a place to sleep. The following day, Mr. Sunshine decided to stay around and help out at the trail angel's house and we planned for me to pick him up after work so he could see my house and where I lived in Vermont. That Thursday morning, I brought him to the trail so that he could start hiking again, but not without planning where I could meet him that night.

I was lucky that Ibex let me change my work schedule during the summer months so that I could work four ten-hour shifts and always have a three-day weekend. For hiking, of course. This meant that after work I could go and meet Mr. Sunshine and hike three more days with him. As it turned out, Sydney, Cucumber, and Joey ended up at the same location on the trail as Mr. Sunshine. The gang was reunited yet again! They had been gifted a free night at an inn as trail magic. The inn was right near Ibex, so that night we all got to stay in comfy, clean beds, and Friday morning, we all piled into my car and got on the trail in Woodstock, Vermont. Once again, I didn't know how I'd get back to my car, but I was confident we'd figure it out. We hiked that weekend to Killington, Vermont. I was able to call my coworker Beth, who lived near there, and asked her to come grab Vaida and me and this hiker guy I just met that I had been telling her all about. Beth was such a sweetheart and promptly picked us up and drove us back to my car in Woodstock.

In order to spend another night together and for Mr. Sunshine to get back on the trail and me to get to work on Monday, we drove my car back to Killington, Vermont and camped together. We wound up doing that mix of meeting Thursday, hiking Friday through Sunday, shuttling back to my car, and camping together the last night a total of five weekends in a row.

As Mr. Sunshine got farther south on the Appalachian Trail, Vaida and I would leave work Thursday night and drive to wherever he was on the trail. We'd hike fifty to sixty miles away and then figure out how to get back to my car together. Once we had the car, we drove back to where we had gotten off the trail. Mr. Sunshine always wanted to come with us so that he could spend one more night with me and Vaida. One time we had an eighty-dollar cab ride, and another time Mr. Sunshine had met someone in a town who offered to drive us from wherever we ended up. Another time we hitchhiked. The last time we did this, someone we had randomly met on the top of a mountain offered to give us a ride. No one ever seemed to have a problem letting a well behaved ninety-pound dog tag along for the ride. It was wild and adventurous. I was never worried. I just somehow knew it would always work out.

When Mr. Sunshine got as far south as Connecticut, the driving logistics became too much. That last Monday morning, I was incredibly sad about not knowing when, or if, I would ever see him again. I was crying. He took the car keys out of my hand and said, "Get in the passenger seat. I'm coming back with you to Vermont, and I'm going to spend the week with you."

Vaida and I hiked 150 miles of the A.T. with Mr. Sunshine that summer. That winter I flew to North Carolina to meet him and hike the last 150 miles of the trail. A few months later, Mr. Sunshine moved from Missouri to Vermont to be with Vaida and me. His real name is Jodeob, mentioned in other fun and venturesome moments I've shared in this book that occurred after our initial meeting. We ended up dating for five years. Although no longer together, we are still close friends and he, too, holds a special place in his heart for Vaida.

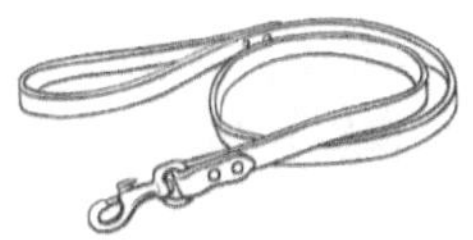

When I was preparing to do the direttissima in the summer of 2016, I was doing a lot of research on it and reading as many reports as I could about past hikers' experiences from those who had completed this massive White Mountains hike. A direttissima is an Italian word that means "most direct route." In New Hampshire's White Mountains, that means one consecutive backpacking trip connecting all forty-eight of the four-thousand-footers. Typically, folks start at Mount Moosilauke and end on Mount Cabot. It's approximately 250 miles with a hundred thousand feet in elevation change. What I really wanted to figure out was the feasibility of doing it with a dog. I had come across a blog written by a woman named Arlette, whose trail name was "Apple Pie." She had completed a direttissima a few years earlier, so I was able to get a lot of information from her blog. The more I read, the more excited I was about getting to attempt this huge undertaking with Vaida.

There was another woman who was really well-known in the hiking community, Heather, aka Anish. She had some incredible hiking feats on many major long-distance trails throughout the country. Of course, I followed her on social media. One day I noticed she posted a picture from the White Mountains with Arlette, and I realized that was the woman whose blog I'd been reading. I had been thinking about trying to get in touch with Arlette, and this felt like the perfect opportunity. I sent Arlette a message, telling her I wanted to learn more about the direttissima.

As it turned out, she lived in Massachusetts and hiked in the White Mountains all the time. She suggested that we get together, so we made plans to meet at The Notch Hostel for tea. She told me about the trip, the difficulty of it, the long days I should expect, and she tried to shed some light on how tough it would be on a dog. I told her that Vaida had a lot of hiking experience, including the 48 as well as many long days and high miles backpacking. She made me feel confident that we could do it.

As I mentioned earlier, I didn't wind up doing it. Between the trail magic I had received on my first day out and the instant friendships I made with Cucumber, Sydney, Joey, and Mr. Sunshine, after just two days I decided to enjoy my vacation rather than drag Vaida 250 miles through the White Mountains. Despite my not completing the direttissima, Arlette and I stayed in touch about various other hiking experiences and adventures. We decided that we should hike together and have since gone on many hikes and become good friends. Her husband, Rich "Greenleaf," is an avid hiker as well, an incredibly experienced long-distance hiker who also knows everything about the White Mountains. They're both older and far more experienced than I am. I really started to look up to both of them for different reasons. Between the two of them, they have over forty thousand long-distance miles logged, eleven thousand of them being logged together. In the summer of 2022, Arlette became the first known woman to hike each of the eleven National Scenic Trails in the country. She's made a name for herself in the long-distance hiking community because of her accomplishments, her humble personality, and her willingness to always share information and help others. She's also really good at hiking incredibly long days, plus she always carries these really cute sock dolls that she makes and loves to share with other hikers.

Rich is known for being able to push miles quickly and on very little sleep, sometimes covering more than fifty miles in one go. In spite of their different hiking styles, they often hike a lot of trails together. They make it work and have this really beautiful relationship. They also support each other in their separate long-distance endeavors, often joining one another for sections at a time. Over the years, I've done a lot of hiking with the two of them. When Arlette was hiking the Colorado Trail in 2017, I was able to join her for 150 miles of that trip. One of my fondest memories of hiking with both Arlette and Rich as well as Vaida was a New Year's Day overnight hike to our favorite cabin in the Northern Presidentials, Gray Knob Cabin. I'm not sure either of them had hiked with dogs much before, but they seemed really impressed by not only Vaida's calm and gentle presence, but her ability to hike across this rugged snow-covered mountain terrain.

To this day, if I have a question about a trail or a hike, I'll count on Arlette and Rich to give me advice. I can't even count the number of times I've been in the middle of a hike in a questionable situation and called them. They always answer their phone. They're really wonderful people, and I'm grateful to have met the two of them and have them in my life. It's not my trail name, but they refer to me as "Grasshopper" because I'm always learning.

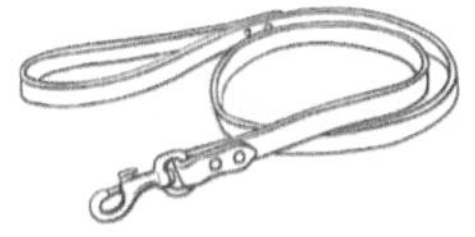

The hiking community not only consists of people you meet at a hostel or while on the trail but also people that you meet through social media. Tom, "The Real Hiking Viking," also known by his trail name, "Jabba," was the first known person to hike the Appalachian Trail southbound from Maine to Georgia starting in the winter. Typically, a southbound A.T. hike starts in Maine in the early summer and you make it to Georgia by the fall. Tom took on the challenge of starting his hike in Maine in December, in the most rugged terrain and the most extreme winter weather conditions possible. He had completed a northbound thru-hike of the A.T. A couple of years earlier, and that's when he discovered the long-distance hiking community and became obsessed. He built a name for himself and became really well-known as "The Real Hiking Viking." That's how I ended up following him on social media, along with more than fifty thousand other followers.

I was working at Ibex when I learned about his winter southbound attempt starting in December of 2015. This was the year I really got into winter hiking in the White Mountains, and I knew what it would take to hike this section of trail in the snow, wind, and cold of winter. It seemed completely out of this world and impossible. Knowing Tom had such a large social media presence, I thought to myself, *Maybe we can help this guy out, and he can help us.* I went to see Ted, the CEO of Ibex, curious to see if he would tell me to reach out to Tom.

I said, "Ted, you won't believe this, but this hiker I follow on Instagram who has fifty thousand followers is trying to hike the entire Appalachian Trail southbound in the winter."

Ted looked at me and said half-jokingly, "He's going to die."

I said, "I know he is going to die." To me, this attempt seemed crazy, not only because of how cold and snowy it is and how it gets dark before five o'clock and that he's living outside, but also some of those trails are not traveled in the winter. He would probably be hiking in several feet of snow, have to dig out a place for his tent before he could set it up, and break through ice or melt snow for water. He could go days without seeing a single other person. It seemed cold, lonely, and incomprehensible to me.

Ted said to me, "Let's send him some Ibex."

I wasn't feeling very confident about contacting this very well-known hiker, and I was sure that now he had made his announcement, he'd have a thousand people trying to reach him. Despite feeling a little unsure and shy, I found his email on his website and sent him a message. I didn't think I'd ever hear back from him, but a couple of hours later, my desk phone rang and I answered.

"Is this Caitlin?"

"Yes."

"It's Tom, The Real Hiking Viking."

I was in shock.

He told me that he would love it if I could send him some Ibex gear and that he would check out the Ibex website. At the time, I was thinking it would be a few items. Maybe a pair of gloves and a hat, some base layers and a midlayer. Later that day, he sent me a list of almost twenty things. I was a little surprised by the quantity but told him I'd see if Ibex was willing to do that. Unsure of how to approach Ted with this request, I sheepishly walked into his office and was honestly a little surprised when he said, "Let's do it. Send him whatever he wants." So that's what I did. I sent Tom a whole bunch of Ibex stuff. I didn't think he'd carry all twenty pieces of wool clothing with him, but I knew he had great options to choose from. Of course, he would be tagging us on social media and all of his followers would now know about Ibex.

Now that I had made contact with Tom, I wanted to stay in touch and help him out if I could. I decided that when he got to Vermont, Vaida and I would love to hike with him for at least a day, offer him a place to stay, and maybe I could bring him to the Ibex headquarters. My friend, Tick Tock, who I had met on my Long Trail hike earlier that year, was working for me at Ibex at the time. She had taken me up on an offer to come live and work in Vermont for the winter so she could gain some winter hiking experience. We had gone on a handful of winter hikes together, and I thought it would be cool if she wanted to join when Vaida and I met Tom.

I always loved spending New Year's Eve at The Notch Hostel, so Tick Tock and I went there to spend the night. From following Tom on social media, I knew that he was in southern Maine, not too far from The Notch and in the back of my mind I was thinking we could use this opportunity to try and find him. I sent Tom a message that night and found out that he was in Andover, Maine, spending New Year's Eve at The Cabin, a hostel run by a couple in their eighties, Honey and Bear. Their hostel was typically only open to A.T. thru-hikers in the summer and closed for the winter. We knew they had opened their doors for Tom, who was attempting this incredible feat, but we weren't sure they would let two random girls and a dog stay there too. With fingers crossed, on New Year's Day I called, and Bear answered.

"Hi, Bear, I'm friends with Tom. He's staying with you. Would it be all right if my friend and I came and visited? I have a dog with me."

Immediately and very sweetly he told me that would be fine. "Honey is making her famous pasta with meat sauce and garlic bread. You, your friend, and your dog are welcome to join."

Hanging up the phone, I felt like I had just finished talking to my eighty-year-old grandparents and couldn't believe we had just been so warmly and kindly invited into their home for dinner. Having been a vegetarian since I was thirteen, I was not so excited about the meat sauce part, but I knew I'd be eating it that night. There was no way I was going to be rude and a picky dinner guest in this sweet old woman's home.

Bear had also told me that Tom was out hiking and the time and place he was going to be picking him up from the trail. This location was only ninety minutes from The Notch, so Tick Tock and I decided this was the perfect opportunity to get a short hike in with Vaida and try to intercept Tom. We headed to the trail an hour before Bear's pickup time in order to hike into the woods and find him. He had no idea we were doing this, so it was a fun way to meet for the very first time. We were probably the first people and for sure the first and only dog he had seen on the A.T. in days, so he was very excited. After we all hung out and chatted for a few minutes, we hiked back to the road together as he shared stories from his first few hundred miles of the trail, and went back to Honey and Bear's place. They welcomed us into their home with open arms. After hours of conversation in their living room, we shared a family-style dinner and chatted for several hours more. I'll never forget that evening, although I don't remember what Vaida did, probably because she just did her normal thing and found somewhere comfy to snooze away.

It was so cool hearing all their stories from owning the hostel for so many years and seeing this huge room that was covered in Appalachian Trail pictures, posters, and signs, like a shrine to the A.T. The next morning, the three of us went out to breakfast in Andover, and then Tick Tock, Vaida, and I left the next day. I told Tom that when he got to New Hampshire to let me know.

It took Tom a few weeks of cold, snowy, difficult hiking to make it to New Hampshire, but after he managed to make it through the

White Mountains, I picked him up in Hanover so he could come to my house for the night. We made a plan to hike ten miles from Hanover, New Hampshire, to West Hartford, Vermont, the following day. He told me his friend, Matt, who lived in Vermont, was going to join us on the hike and that we would be able to leave a car in both locations. I was surprised to hear he had a friend in Vermont, so I asked him how they knew each other. He told me that he knew him from the music festival circuit because they went to a lot of live music together. Having spent so many years working in the music industry, I had this sneaking suspicion that maybe I too knew Matt. When Tom showed me a picture of Matt, I was totally shocked. I did know the guy! But I didn't know him from the music scene. I had met him the previous winter, when my friend Mason was teaching me how to backcountry ski. Matt was learning too. What a small world.

Before our hike in the morning, we all went out to breakfast at a famous A.T. breakfast spot called Lou's. I got to see Matt for the first time in at least a year. Tick Tock, Matt, Tom, Vaida, and I all hiked the ten-mile section from Hanover to West Hartford, telling stories and sharing laughs the entire way. After the hike, Matt and I exchanged numbers and have since shared many memorable hikes together. He's told me that some of his most favorite winter hikes have been with Vaida and me.

Tom spent a second night on my couch, and we stayed up super late that night talking about hiking, my eighties wrestling figure collection, and playing old original Nintendo games. The next morning, he planned to go to Randy and Linda's house for breakfast, well-known trail angels who live in West Hartford, Vermont. I was excited that I got to meet and experience these trail angels I had heard so much about and enjoy their massive hiker breakfast. With a full belly, Tom went on his way.

Tom and I have remained in touch over the years. Ironically, in the summer of 2021 I ran into him again in Andover, Maine of all places, when I was hiking a five-hundred-mile section of the A.T. Tom was not hiking but actually supporting a fellow well-known ultrarunner, Scott Jurek, who at one time held the fastest known time for hiking the A.T. Scott was attempting to break the existing record, and Tom was driving one of the crew vehicles that was providing food, water, and whatever else Scott needed. It was great to see Tom after five years and briefly catch up. The hiking community is composed of a vast network of people, yet this random meeting was a reminder of how connected we really can be.

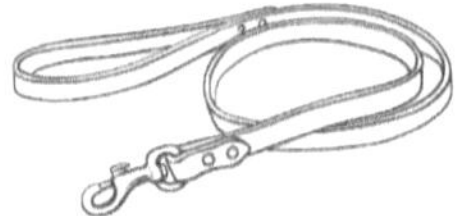

In addition to all the individual hikers who have touched my and Vaida's lives, a family of hikers stands out—Kami and Ben Crawford and their six children. In 2018, the Crawfords, with children ranging in age from two to sixteen, became the largest family ever to hike the Appalachian Trail. They have a popular YouTube channel that documents their life at home, their unique educational practices, and their many family adventures. One of their most challenging adventures was deciding to thru-hike the Appalachian Trail in 2018 as a family. Vaida and I had the pleasure of meeting and spending time with them during that hike.

I first learned about the Crawfords a few days after they had started their hike in Georgia. I saw a post about them on one of the many hiking social media pages I follow and was immediately intrigued. As I've opened up more over the years, I've noticed that I always seem to reach out to people when I find out they're doing something seemingly wild, crazy, or out of the ordinary. So it was only natural that I wanted to meet the Crawfords. I wanted to be friends with them, so I sent them a message telling them, "I live in Vermont right near the Appalachian Trail. When you guys get farther north, let me know. I think what you're doing is incredible."

Being so intrigued by this family of eight attempting to hike the entire A.T., Jodeob and I started watching their daily YouTube updates from the trail almost religiously. In the beginning, Jodeob said, "There's no way they're going to make it. They've got a two-year-old and a big family. There's just no way." But every day, he would get a little more optimistic. "Maybe they really are going to do it." Before we knew it, they were halfway. The next thing we knew, they were almost to Vermont. I messaged them, asking to keep me posted when they got closer. They let me know when they got to Killington, Vermont, which was only thirty miles from where we lived.

Even though I hadn't seen any updates from them for a few days and I wasn't sure exactly where they were, I had this gut feeling that if

Jodeob, Vaida, and I went to West Hartford, Vermont, and walked south for a few miles, we'd run into them that day. With confidence and excitement, Jodeob and I filled a backpack with a variety of drinks, including soda and chocolate milk, which was their youngest's favorite, and a beer for Ben and Kami. It was my turn to hand out trail magic.

We started hiking, and sure enough, after a short time, we began to run into some of the Crawford children. Appearing to be in a rush, they politely declined our refreshment offers, telling us that they were late to meet someone. They also didn't seem to notice, or care, about our ninety-pound yellow friend who was with us, Vaida.

Finally, we saw Ben and Kami walking toward us with one of the other children and the youngest on their back.

I said, "Ben and Kami, it's Caitlin and Jodeob. We brought you guys drinks." Vaida, Jodeob, and I wound up getting to walk three or four miles with them and chat about their decision to hike the trail and the difficulties they'd faced so far. They were such inspiring people.

Knowing the White Mountains were not too far ahead, when we were saying our goodbyes, I told them that we would be more than happy to help them out if they needed anything. I also really wanted to spend more time with them. That night Kami messaged me and said, "Hey, Caitlin, Friday is Ben's birthday and we're going to be coming down Mount Moosilauke. If I send you a list of all his favorite food, could you bring it? I'll give you money." Of course I said, "Absolutely."

That Friday, we got everything on Kami's list and Jodeob and I went to the parking lot at the base of Mount Moosilauke. We set up a small grill and within a half hour of us getting there, the family came marching down the trail. Ben was so surprised. They were joined by some of their other trail friends known as "The Degenerates." There were also some other random thru-hikers who happily joined in on the celebration. Even Serena came up from The Notch Hostel and joined us. We had a big birthday party with fifteen to twenty hikers in the parking lot. As the party wound down, Ben and Kami told me they were planning on camping there that night. We had made a plan with them for the next day to slack pack a sixteen-mile section over what's called "the Kinsmans." They would leave all of their overnight gear with Jodeob so they only had to carry day-packs, and I was going to join them. By this time, because of the heat, we were limiting Vaida's summertime hiking, so she would stay behind with Jodeob and go swimming. When Serena learned they were going to camp in the parking lot, she insisted that they come back to the hostel as it was only five miles down the road. The family happily piled into our two cars and headed to the hostel.

The next day, we hiked the sixteen miles and had so much fun. It was really special watching their family dynamics and learning more about their trip thus far and how each child had a role. Their thirteen-year-old son was their media guy. He carried a camera and a computer. Whenever they got to a town, he was in charge of uploading and editing their YouTube videos. Each of the girls was in charge of a meal. They had to do the shopping for the food and once they were on the trail, they would prepare and hand it out to the rest of the family. When they got to camp, the kids had to set up the tents while the parents took care of the youngest child, Rainier. They were not just having their children come on this trip, they were really making them a part of it, including the planning. Ben, Kami, and the three oldest Crawford children shared responsibility for carrying two-year-old Rainier as well as hiking gear in a special child-carrying backpack weighing upward of fifty-five pounds with him in it.

Following that day's hike, Jodeob and I took them out to dinner. During dinner, they debated whether they could make it to Katahdin, the northern terminus, by a certain date, because they had promised their children that they could go to their favorite summer camp. They only had three weeks to get there, and it was almost four hundred miles away. Being the most difficult section of the entire trail due to the elevation gain and loss, this seemed relatively daunting, but we tried to convince them they could do it.

Jodeob and I both agreed, "You guys have made it this far. You've been doing twenty miles a day. You can do it."

We were supposed to go back home to Vermont the next day because we ran a roadside barbecue business on Sundays. I begged Jodeob to hike one more day with them because they were going over Franconia Ridge, one of my favorite sections of trail in New Hampshire. He agreed and said that he would take Vaida swimming again. She got to hang out with the Crawfords at Ben's party in the parking lot and did the short hike in Vermont to meet them, but at that point, she was retired from summer hiking. I was pleased that I got to spend one more day with the family on one of my favorite sections of the White Mountains.

After having spent two full days hiking with the Crawford family, what impressed me the most was the camaraderie, positivity, and determination of all eight family members no matter the circumstances. The Crawfords were a seemingly ordinary group of folks doing a very inspiring and extraordinary thing.

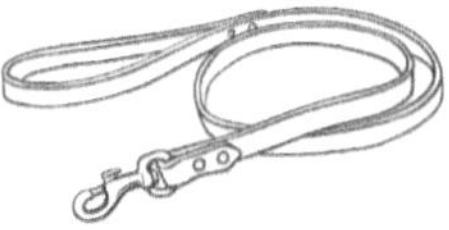

When I think about the hiking community, I think about my introduction to it in the summer of 2016 and about The Notch Hostel. It was that summer when Vaida and I first dove into the White Mountains and the NH48, and from there, we slowly started becoming known at The Notch and slowly started making friends with regulars. We were also becoming recognized on the trails of the 48, which was weird for me. I wasn't used to the attention or folks actually wanting to have a conversation with me. But I also realized that the reason people recognized me was because of the beautiful, well-behaved ninety-pound yellow dog by my side. Guests at the hostel and hikers on the trail couldn't help but want to stop and talk to me. As time went on and more and more people stopped me, I gradually became more talkative and outgoing. The feelings of being a rookie hiker dissipated as I gained recognition as a White Mountains hiker, and my confidence level grew. I remain convinced to this day that were it not for the fact that I was known as the girl with the big yellow dog, I would have not stood out and had the opportunity to meet amazing individuals in the hiking community.

9

Not-So-Perfect Adventures

There's never a dull day on the trail, but sometimes things can get really strange. Often Vaida's and my experiences were unpredictable by design. I can't tell you how many times we'd finish a day of hiking without a clear plan for the next day. We spent most of our weekends at The Notch Hostel in North Woodstock, New Hampshire. If I didn't have a clear plan in the morning, my decision was often based on either the weather, a conversation I'd had the previous night with another guest about their hiking plans, the advice of Justin and Serena, or a combination of all of these things.

That was the case with Peter, an older gentleman I met at The Notch. He was working on finishing his NH48 and was a regular guest there. I had chatted with him before, but I'd never hiked with him. When he told me he was going to hike Mount Monroe the next day, which is just under two miles from Mount Washington, I decided Vaida and I would join him. The trail we were going to use takes you up to Lakes of the Clouds Hut, which is one of eight huts in the White Mountains operated by the Appalachian Mountain Club. The huts provide a place where hikers can get out of the elements, take a break, get some water, or spend the night for a fee. Three of the eight huts are open year-round, and while Lakes of the Clouds is not one of them, the benches outside provide a great place to relax for a few minutes before continuing your hike.

Lakes of the Clouds Hut is the highest Appalachian Mountain Club hut, sitting above-tree-line just over five thousand feet and located in the saddle between Mount Washington and Mount Monroe. Using the most standard route, people typically hike three miles up Ammonoosuc Ravine Trail, take a break at the hut, and then hike a half mile to the summit of Mount Monroe. Once you hike the half mile back down to the hut, it's only a mile and a half to the summit of Mount Washington, and you can hike the Jewell Trail down and end up back at your car. This loop route is a great way to hike Mount Monroe and Mount Washington, which is the highest peak in the Northeast.

When Peter told me he was "just" hiking Monroe, I thought about the fact that normally people use the loop route and hike Mount Washington too, but I understood that adding Washington can be an undertaking because of the extra miles, extra elevation gain, and prolonged above-tree-line exposure. But I was just happy to hike with someone else, so I said, "Sure, let's go for it." It was early December, so it wasn't the dead of winter, at least not down in the valley and at the hostel, but waking up that morning, I had a bit of an eerie feeling. The day looked overcast, like it was going to snow and mother nature had woken up on the wrong side of the bed.

We had been hiking in winter-like conditions and on snow-covered trails since the beginning of November, so I was well prepared. I knew the trail itself would be snow-packed because it was such a popular winter route, and that around us would be deeper snow. It was going to be a very white, snowy landscape. I was wearing my merino wool mid- and base layers, had extra layers, goggles, and both my Gore-Tex and down jackets packed. Vaida wore her thick yellow "fur" coat. I would hike in my insulated winter boots and wear microspikes for traction. Yet still, something felt off.

I can't remember why, but for some reason we drove separately to the trailhead. We left the hostel and drove through Franconia Notch. As I was driving, I noticed that it was getting darker and had started to snow, and the feeling I had woken up with was getting worse. But hiking in the snow wasn't anything Peter, Vaida, or I were afraid of and we had made this plan, so we were determined to go for it, knowing we could always bail.

When we got to the parking lot, it wasn't snowing nearly as much as it had been in Franconia Notch. This made sense, as the weather in the notch can often be far worse than in other areas down in the valley. We geared up and were excited to start the hike. At that point, I didn't have that eerie feeling anymore. The weather forecast was simply calling for overcast skies and seasonal temperatures. I was ready to go. I thought it would be a fun day. Peter suggested that Vaida and I hike ahead of him, but I said, "No, we made this plan. Let's hike together." Again, he said, "You're younger and you're stronger and you've hiked more than me. It's no problem if you want to hike ahead." But I insisted, and we started hiking together, with Vaida ambling along slightly ahead as usual.

We were chatting and having a good time and enjoying our snowy surroundings. The weather didn't seem bad. Every now and then I noticed I was getting a little bit ahead of him, so I'd stop and wait a couple of minutes. He'd catch back up. He'd catch his breath and say, "Caitlin, you don't have to wait for me. Go ahead." I would hike with him for a little bit and then Vaida and I would once again end up ahead. Then we'd stop, and he'd show up a few minutes later. This happened three or four times.

Sometimes if it's cold, you need to keep your body moving in order to maintain your increased heart rate, which is what's keeping you warm. You can't wait for the person behind you. But it wasn't that cold, so whenever I got ahead, I didn't worry about stopping and waiting. When I got approximately one mile from Lakes of the Clouds Hut, I decided I would hike up to the hut and wait for him there. Once I was within one hundred feet of the hut, everything around me was white and I could barely make out the outline of the hut in the distance. I had been in conditions like this plenty of times before, so rather than feeling nervous, I was starting to get excited.

Vaida marched along ahead of me, and when we arrived at the hut, I couldn't see Mount Monroe even though it was only a half mile away. Now that we were above-tree-line, the weather had changed from a relaxing, overcast hike in the trees to a complete whiteout. Somehow it was still very exhilarating. It wasn't snowing very hard, but the clouds and weather had definitely moved in. With my heart rate still up, it didn't feel that cold yet, but it was cold enough, and it was windy, snow on the ground was blowing, and I could not see much in front of me because of the cloud cover. I've always really enjoyed being in these somewhat intense winter conditions. It's such an experience to be in a place that you've also enjoyed dozens of times under bright, sunny summer skies, the scenery shining blue and green instead a complete whiteout blanketed in snow. I had grown comfortable in all hiking conditions, and I think Vaida had too because as the snow collected on the tips of her fur and her "ice beard" began to grow, she simply found a nice snowy spot to lie down and clear the balls of snow that had collected between the pads of her paws.

While we were waiting outside the hut for Peter, out of nowhere, a hiker and his dog came from the other side of the hut, from the direction of Mount Washington.

Surprised, I said, "Did you just come from Mount Washington?! Because this is really intense." The wind had picked up and the visibility had decreased even more. Snow was being blown all across the trail.

He introduced himself, telling me his name was Howie, and said, "No way. I was just in the dungeon under the hut."

I'd never been in the dungeon before, but I knew it was a small, unheated cement basement that at least allowed you to escape the cold temperatures, snow, and wind and warm up a bit. It was accessed through an outside doorway on the side of the hut and was primarily used for emergencies and had a couple of bunk beds in it. The reason Howie could get into it was because it was only December and the building hadn't been buried in snow yet. As winter progresses, you can't use the dungeon because the snow drifts cover the entrance and the metal door freezes shut. Howie asked me if I wanted to go check it out, warm up a bit, and get out of the whiteout. I said I was waiting for a friend, but he said I should go in and at least get out of the wind. After a few minutes, we could come back out and check for Peter. It was nice to get out of the elements and warm up for a bit and for Vaida to have a chance to thaw out all of the frozen snow blanketing her fur. It was also neat to check out the dungeon since I had never been in there. It was small—you could probably cram a dozen people in there if you had to, but only six or so could sleep in it.

There were other people in there escaping the elements as well, two gentlemen who were hiking together, plus a couple of college-age guys with their father. The boys were wearing jeans and cotton sweatshirts, which is definitely not the ideal hiking attire, especially for those conditions. Despite the gusty, snowy conditions and lack of visibility, because the two boys and their father had come all the way from Boston to hike Mount Washington, they were determined to do it. Shortly after we arrived in the dungeon, they shouted, "Washington or bust!" and opened the door, exposing the whipping wind and blowing snow. They weren't going to be able to see anything or find the trail, and I knew they were definitely not going up Mount Washington. Not surprisingly, they came back a few minutes later exclaiming how crazy it was outside.

Meanwhile, I said to Howie that Peter had to be coming up soon and I needed to head out so he would know where I was. Howie said he was ready to hike down the mountain and would go with me, so we left the dungeon. Unfortunately, Peter was not at the hut yet and I began to wonder if he had either already turned around when he saw the conditions or was still making his way up the trail. If that was the case and Howie and I started hiking down, surely we would find Peter. There was just one problem. We couldn't find the trail. You couldn't see much farther than forty feet, and the wind had blown the snow over our footprints from our hike up. Howie started walking off in one direction to look for the trail, and I tried to stop him, saying, "No, I think the trail is this way, to the right." Howie thought it was to the left, so we were going back and forth about where the trail was. Meanwhile, Vaida just followed along after me, content to be wherever I was. A few minutes later, I saw Peter's bright red coat off in the distance and yelled down to him, asking him if he was on the trail. He said, "Yes," so I said, "Good, stay there."

Howie and I walked down to Peter, and by the look in his eyes, I could tell he already knew there was no way we were going to summit Mount Monroe. We decided we would go back down the mountain by retracing Peter's steps. That's when Howie suggested that we take Peter into the dungeon to warm up for a few minutes before heading down. I was not too excited about this suggestion because Howie and I had spent the past ten minutes trying to find the trail and here we all were now, standing on it. I knew any time spent in the dungeon would blow more snow over the footsteps we had just made. Unfortunately, by this time, Peter needed a break, so he said, "Sure, let's go to the dungeon."

We went back to the dungeon, and the other hikers were still there. After telling everyone about our difficulty finding the trail, we made a group decision to all hike down the mountain together. It was me, Peter, Vaida, Howie and his dog, the two boys and their dad, and the two other gentlemen. We all ran into the same exact issue. No one could find the trail. Even though Howie, Peter, and I had just been on it a few minutes earlier, the whiteout conditions were disorienting and the wind had completely blown it over. Everyone was going in different directions, trying to find it. For some weird reason, just as Howie did earlier, everyone kept thinking it was to the left, and I was adamant that it was to the right. I'm not exactly sure why I was so sure, but I was definitely sure. Probably because I had just been standing on it with Howie and Peter ten minutes prior. Because we were working as a group and agreed to stay together, we were all following whoever was in the lead. At one point, the two gentlemen started walking far to the left, and the next thing you knew, they were falling into spruce traps, which is when the snow is higher than the short spruce trees. They were sinking up to their knees, but they were still wanting to go in that direction. I kept thinking to myself, *This is fucking ridiculous! This can't be the trail when we're finding spruce traps.* I was starting to get a little agitated and nervous, especially because we were expending so much energy, the dogs included.

At that point, it had been at least thirty minutes. It was probably only one-thirty in the afternoon, but we couldn't find the trail. Thoughts of a potential mountain rescue began to enter my mind. I turned to Peter and said, "This is getting kind of scary." He told me that if we couldn't find the trail, we could spend the night in the dungeon. I had a warm jacket and warm layers, but I didn't have a sleeping bag or anything like that. Peter assured me that we would all be able to keep each other warm.

After spending another fifteen minutes trying to find the trail, I finally said to Peter, "If we don't find the trail in the next fifteen minutes, I'm not screwing around anymore. We're going to the dungeon and hope that tomorrow the conditions are better and we can get down this mountain." At that point, I had given up on paying attention to what the other guys were doing. For the most part, they were following each other and getting nowhere. I just turned off and searched for the trail myself with Vaida in tow. I knew it was in the direction opposite of where everyone else was looking. As soon as Vaida and I started walking down to the right, sure enough, from afar, I saw two hikers coming up the mountain. I shouted out and asked them if they were on the trail. When they said, "Yes," I ran over.

As a group we had been up there searching for the trail for an hour. We were cold and bundled up in all our layers. We hadn't been moving very far or very fast. The two hikers, on the other hand, were in long-sleeve shirts, looking very comfortable and warm. They had been going up the mountain for the past two hours and just broken tree line with their heartrates still up. When they saw me in all my layers, frantic, and I told them I was thrilled that they were on the trail, they looked at me like I was crazy. I think I gave the girl a hug.

I warned them that if they went into the dungeon, they needed to be careful when they left because they, too, could lose the trail. I waved the rest of the group over, and we all headed down the mountain, very relieved when we made it back into the trees and out of the elements. The other folks from the dungeon lagged behind a little bit, but Howie, Peter, the two dogs, and I made it down pretty quickly.

Peter and I were both relieved to finally be making our way back to the hostel, but this wild adventure didn't end with the hike. Temperatures had dropped in Franconia Notch, and it was snowing worse than it had been in the morning. As soon as we reached the safety of the parking lot, Peter left to go back to the hostel, and Howie and I hung out for quite a while chatting. By the time I got on the highway and approached Franconia Notch, traffic was at a standstill. It was at this point that I got a knot in the pit of my stomach and had a feeling something bad had happened to Peter. He was ahead of me on the road, and when I called his phone, he didn't answer. I called the hostel, and he wasn't back yet. The knot in my stomach grew.

After an hour of being stuck in standstill traffic, I was starting to run out of gas and had to pee really badly. I wanted to keep the car running to keep Vaida and me warm and also to keep the snow off my wind-shield, but I had to do something. I called the hostel again and spoke to the owner, Justin, curious if he could bring me some gas, but it just wasn't feasible, given the southbound lanes I was in were stopped and he couldn't just stop on the interstate in the northbound lanes. I'm not sure how I came up with my next idea, and it certainly wasn't something I would have done in the past had I not learned to become so innovative over the past few years of hiking with Vaida. First, I found a Ziploc bag to take care of the smaller situation and then I turned the car off, got out, and went up to the SUV behind me. The gentleman driving rolled down his window and, feeling like a bit of a crazy lady, I explained that I was going to run out of gas if I didn't turn my car off until traffic was moving again and asked if I could sit in his car. He said to me, "Of course you can come sit with us, but first, if you have a blanket, you should put it on your windshield to keep the snow off." I thought that was a genius idea. I felt bad taking the blanket from Vaida, but I knew she would be fine in the cold car for a bit. The SUV had a family of four in it that had come up to New Hampshire from Boston for the weekend to ski. While the two kids played in the way back, entertaining themselves by building a fort, I told the husband and wife all about my wild day. I also told them that I had a feeling my hiking companion Peter was involved in why we were in this standstill traffic.

I sat with the family for almost an hour before traffic finally started moving again and I was able to make it to the first highway exit and to a gas station. The family was so nice they even followed me there to be sure I made it okay. It was at the gas station that I learned nine cars had gone off the road in Franconia Notch. Right then and there, I knew Peter had to have been one of them. Had I left behind him, I probably would have gone off the road too, but I'd stayed in the parking lot talking to Howie. When I got back to the hostel, Peter still wasn't there. A few minutes later, his daughter called and said Peter was in the hospital. He had gone off the road in Franconia Notch, just as I had feared. Luckily, Peter only suffered from a few bumps and bruises, a totaled truck, and the intensity of the whiteout conditions near Mount Monroe. While Vaida seemed to have had a typical day on the mountain, for me, this was one of the scariest moments of our hiking to date.

Winter hiking is a unique experience, unlike anything most experience on a typical hike in any other season. It can be simultaneously exhilarating and life-threatening. That day I learned the importance of not only being well prepared for the day's conditions, but also to always be prepared to spend the night in the mountains. It also reminded me that it's okay to turn around. It's okay to not achieve your intended goal. The mountains will be there tomorrow.

Some of the best advice I can offer related to this comes from my good friend Arlette. Besides her incredible achievement as the first woman in the country to ever hike every National Scenic Trail, she is also a very experienced all-season guide. Arlette says, "The most important skill to have to keep you safe while hiking is to know when to bail. In winter specifically, take a moment to check the conditions when you're popping out above-tree-line. Do you have the right gear to stay warm when you no longer have the protection of the trees? Can you see the trail? Are the wind gusts going to blow you around or create a life-threatening wind chill? If any of the conditions make you doubt your safe return, turn around. If you are going to be above-tree-line for a longer time, map out your bailout routes. If conditions deteriorate, are there other trails that can get you off the ridge sooner? The margin of error is so small in winter conditions. Sometimes it's not safe to be out there."

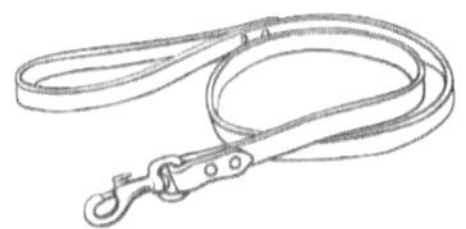

By 2016, I had been three-season day hiking for just over ten years and long-distance backpacking and winter hiking for almost two. Vaida had been hiking with me for the past seven years. Both of us having acquired a ton of miles and also a ton of hiking experience, we had managed to avoid any physical trauma or injury (except for Dead Toe, of course). This was about to change right at the end of our pursuit of the NH48. I planned a long day hike that would cover six four-thousand-foot mountains Vaida and I still needed to check off. It was a twenty-mile traverse that typically requires a car spot, but I was confident Vaida and I could just hitchhike back to my car. The traverse included the Wildcats (Wildcat A and Wildcat D), the Carters (Carter Dome, South Carter, and Middle Carter) and Mount Moriah. The plan was to go up the Polecat ski trail to Wildcat D, then hike across on the Wildcat Ridge Trail to Wildcat A, and then take the Carter-Moriah Trail to all three Carters, do a short out and back to Mount Moriah, hike down the mountain, and find a ride back to my car.

It was the beginning of May, the weather was definitely warming up in the valleys where snow had mostly melted, and things were greening up. However, this was not the case on the trails in the higher elevations. There was still plenty of snow and ice, especially in the areas with low sun exposure. Even on the more exposed sections of trails that enjoyed melting daytime temperatures, it often refroze in the colder nighttime temperatures. One of the things I did, especially in the spring and winter, was always read trip reports online where people post their experiences on the trails from their recent hikes. They talk about traction needed: like microspikes, crampons, or snowshoes; and what the trails were like: snow-packed, icy, or granular. Because I had never done this hike before and knew there was still snow and ice on the mountains, I made sure to read the reports about the twenty-mile stretch I had planned. All of the reports I read were saying how terrible the conditions were and how icy it was.

A few weeks earlier, I'd met a girl who lived across the street from Mount Moriah, near the trail I was planning on hiking down. She was also a very avid White Mountains hiker and was very familiar with the terrain. After having read the recent trip reports, I decided to ask her if she knew what the current conditions were. She told me that it was probably going to be very icy and the traverse wasn't a good idea. I told her that I really wanted to hike these six peaks. I'd even changed my work schedule at Ibex because I saw really good weather in the forecast calling for sunny skies and sixty-degree temperatures. I was so determined to do this hike with Vaida that I also decided to email the woman who had written the most recent trip report I had read. I had never previously contacted people who made these reports, but something told me to email this woman and ask about conditions. She wrote me and said it was really icy and she wouldn't recommend doing it. I was staying at The Notch Hostel the night before and remember going to bed that night thinking, *I just don't know if this is a good idea.*

In the morning, I decided that because I had taken the day off and already driven to the Whites, I was going to go anyway. So Vaida and I took off up Wildcat Mountain. We made it up the ski trail, no problem. We made it over the Wildcats with no problem. When we came to the Carters, we came across some very precarious, very icy sections. If the ice and snow hadn't been there, it would have required navigating down steep piles of large rocks and boulders using my hands and precise foot placement to safely descend the six- to ten-foot pitches.

But in this case, those rocks were covered with smooth, slippery frozen bulges of ice. Temperatures were still cold at night at four thousand feet, so as the remaining snow melted, it added to the already formed frozen runoff. There was no way to go around them, because there was a rocky mountain to the left and a steep drop-off into a bunch of trees and deep snow on the right. Moving slowly, with caution, Vaida and I made it across some pretty problematic sections. I could feel my heart rate starting to elevate, but Vaida seemed to cross them with ease. It was as if the ice wasn't even there. I was always in awe of how she could just lumber across, up, or down parts of the trail that required a lot of thought, attention, and care on my part. As I crossed them, I thought, *There is no way, even if I wanted to, to turn around.* There was no way I was going to get back up some of those steep icy sections, and I wasn't sure Vaida would be able to either. We had to keep going. So we did.

When I got to the third six-foot ice bulge, I was really freaked out. Even though I was wearing microspikes, which grab the ice well, I didn't have crampons, which have larger spikes and are designed to really dig into the ice, especially on steeper slopes. I was in running shorts and running shoes with the microspikes. I stared for a couple minutes at this big slide of ice I had to get down. Vaida was just sitting there while I was staring at it. I couldn't go to the left. I couldn't go to the right. I guess I had no choice. I knew I had to get down it.

As I lifted up my right foot to begin my descent, my left foot suddenly flew out from under me and I was airborne. I was going down the bulge, but not the way I had planned. I was hoping my spikes would have enough traction, but instead I was midair from the top to the bottom. Fortunately, or unfortunately, there was a tree at the bottom of the steep ice bulge, seven or eight inches wide, that stopped me. I hit the tree hard and ended up with one leg on each side of the tree. Thankfully, I didn't hit my head.

I stood up and was in intense pain after the hard impact. I thought to myself, *Holy shit, I think I just broke my vagina!* I took a deep breath and wiped my forehead and thought to myself, *Wow, I'm actually okay.* Then I noticed on my right hand there was a small splotch of blood. I was feeling the effects of the impact on my pelvis, but nothing else hurt. I looked down at my left leg and saw a huge gash a couple of inches long, split wide open, on the inner side of my thigh. I could see through the layers of skin, fat, and muscle, there was a hole in my leg, a long, wide hole. It was covered in dirt and debris from the tree, and it was disgusting. A broken branch on the tree that stopped my fall must have gotten me. I grabbed my backpack, took a shirt out of it, and tied it around my leg as tight as I could. I didn't know much about wilderness first aid, but I'd seen in movies that you tie stuff around body parts that might bleed. It was so deep it wasn't actively bleeding, but it was a big open wound. The pain in my pelvis dissipated as my focus shifted to this huge gash, which luckily didn't hurt but definitely needed medical attention.

I turned around and looked back up at the evil ice bulge where Vaida was standing and said to Vaida, "Let's go!" She didn't budge. I had to reach up and help her down. I immediately started hiking. I knew I wasn't going to go up Moriah and that I had to get down off the mountain. I also knew I had about six miles to hike and, when I got down, I wouldn't be at my car. Hitchhiking no longer seemed an option because I needed immediate help, so I called Serena at The Notch Hostel hoping she could come get me. I needed to get to the hospital as soon as possible. Unfortunately, she was in Boston visiting her parents, but she assured me she could make some calls and find me a ride.

Serena's mom was a nurse and she put her on the phone. Her mom said, "It's okay, honey. Just breathe, drink some water, eat a snack." When Serena got back on the phone, she told me that she knew a gentleman who gave hikers rides and lived in the area and that she would call him. Within a few minutes, she called me back saying he would be waiting for me. I don't think I ever hiked so fast in my life. I was running on pure adrenaline and covered those six miles in under two hours. Vaida was able to keep up the pace and, other than the fact that we were moving a little faster than normal, I don't think she sensed anything was wrong. Or maybe she did and instinctively knew how much I depended on her calmness.

In my rush to get down the mountain, I called my mom, though I was a little hesitant. She didn't know I was hiking that day. I always told my mom or a friend my plans because I wanted someone to know where Vaida and I were going, but on that particular day, she wasn't the one I had told. I had told a friend instead. My mom used to be the person I always shared my plans with, but once I started hiking so much, I finally had to have the conversation with her that it might not always be her. The very first thing I said was, "Mom, I'm okay." And then I proceeded to tell her what had happened and that I couldn't talk because I needed to get down the mountain and to a hospital.

When I finally got down to the trailhead, the gentleman Serena had called was there waiting for me. He asked me what happened, and when I showed him my leg, he said, "You need to go to the hospital now," and offered to take me there immediately. I declined his offer because I wanted to be sure Vaida stayed with me. I knew I could drive myself to the hospital and that Vaida would be more comfortable relaxing in her own car while I was being seen. Because I was so insistent, he took me to my car, wished me luck, and off Vaida and I went to the hospital. I got eight stitches.

The next day at Ibex, my coworker Junior told me I could have hit my femoral artery. I didn't even know what that was. He said, "Caitlin, it's *only* the most important artery in your entire body. If you had hit that, you would have bled out and died within minutes." Hearing that was pretty alarming. I was devastated that I had made such a mistake, putting myself at such risk, as well as Vaida, but I knew all I could do was learn from it.

Some might question why I ignored the warnings about the trail conditions and decided to try that twenty-mile traverse anyway. I had never been on any of those trails or mountain peaks before. I was going in blind, and I was also being stubborn. I could have waited a week or two. The snow and ice would have melted. It would have been better, safer. But I only had a few weeks if I wanted to complete the NH48 in one year. I saw a sixty-five-degree day in May with blue skies in the forecast. It seemed to be a perfect day to do a twenty-mile hike to check those six peaks off my list. Several people told me that I shouldn't take that hike and the websites that I used all indicated conditions were far from ideal to do it. Nothing had stopped me and Vaida thus far. I had winter hiking experience but hadn't experienced extreme spring ice conditions. In retrospect, it wasn't such a great idea, and I know better for next time.

Because of the accident, I still needed to hike Mount Moriah. I also had three other peaks remaining before completing the NH48. The following weekend, with stitches in my leg, Vaida and I hiked those final four peaks. I call that scar my "48 scar."

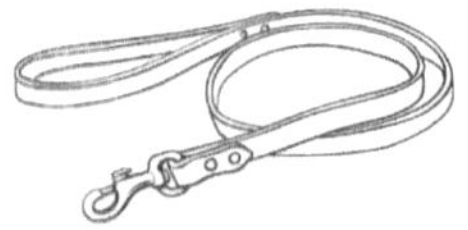

The Mount Monroe hike with Peter and the evil ice bulge accident are two vivid memories of my time spent in the White Mountains. A potential mountain rescue and a trip to the hospital make them especially noteworthy. Luckily, they are the only two times I recall actually fearing for the worst. Thankfully, I could go on and on and on recalling all of the incredible memories of being on those mountains with Vaida. We would hike every weekend, because there was always a four-thousand-footer to climb, people to meet, and experiences to be had. Winter hikes are some of the most memorable, even though hiking in the winter can require a lot of planning and navigating weather and conditions. That didn't stop Vaida and me. It didn't matter that it was winter or that it was snowy or cold, we learned to always be prepared and know when it was time to turn around.

Believe it or not, as long as you have the right gear, knowledge, and experience, hiking in the winter is arguably easier than hiking in other seasons. As the snow fills in the trails, you no longer have to worry about roots and rocks and staircases formed by the natural terrain. All you have to do is hike up a steep snow-packed trail. Because winter hiking in the White Mountains is so popular, the most traveled trails stay packed down the majority of the winter, making them almost like snow-covered sidewalks. They just go up a mountain instead of lying flat.

So many of my memories being in windy or whiteout conditions on top of snow-covered landscapes were special because I was there with Vaida. We knew these landscapes in other seasons, but seeing them in winter, blanketed in white, was incredibly beautiful. I especially loved those crisp, cold days when Vaida's fur was tipped in white and she developed an "ice beard." The cold and snow never seemed to faze her. It might as well have been summer. She just ambled along like normal. When we stopped to take a break along the way, to eat a snack, or add or take off a layer, Vaida would lie down and patiently wait. As soon as I would put my pack back on, she would get up and continue ambling up the trail. There are so many things to enjoy when it comes to winter hiking. The excitement of getting to the top of a mountain, the beautiful contrast of the white snow against the cloudless, bright blue sky, rime ice on signs, or simply what you went through to get to the summit. It didn't matter if I was hiking with friends, or doing a solo hike with Vaida, her routine when she got to the top was always the same. She would sit for a moment and take in the view, then lie down to nap while I, and any friends who hiked with us, marveled at the beautiful views, snapped pictures, and carried on in excitement. Vaida slept through it all.

Mount Moosilauke was always one of my favorite mountains. There's at least a quarter mile that is completely above-tree-line. There aren't huge rocks and boulders like on Franconia Ridge or in the Presidential Range, and I always felt like we were walking on the moon. I have dozens and dozens of recollections of hiking that mountain in the winter with Vaida. Depending on the weather conditions, often the only way to follow the trail was by following piles of rocks placed along the way. These piles are called cairns, and when visibility was low because it was overcast, windy, and the snow was blowing, this was the only way to stay on the trail. Vaida never seemed to notice changes in temperature or conditions. She didn't care if you could see or not see. She knew these mountains about as well as I did. She took the lead, like always, and ambled along following the cairns. It truly amazed me how, no matter what, she could follow a trail. I never quite figured it out, often wondering if it was because she could smell or sense the thousands of people who had trodden the trail ahead over the years. Even if it was well below freezing or even well below zero degrees, snowing, and forty-mile-an-hour winds, it was as if she simply understood that following the trail was what we were doing that day.

Not much else about hiking fazed Vaida either—not other hikers, nor their dogs, or even wildlife. She wasn't a squirrel or chipmunk chaser, and apparently, she wasn't a moose chaser either. I had seen plenty of moose on the side of the road while driving, but I'd never seen one while hiking in the woods. In April, as I was nearing completion of the New Hampshire 48, that changed. Vaida and I had plans to hike the two not-so-popular mountains on the list, Waumbek and Cabot. Normally, people do these as two separate hikes on two separate days. I knew there was a cabin on Cabot where we could stay, so I wanted to combine them and do them as an overnight hike and stay at the cabin. This required hiking Kilkenny Ridge, a section of trail between the two mountains that is not very widely used. It was pretty boring, just the woods and not many views of anything. What I did start seeing, though, were piles of moose poop about every six feet. I was getting bored and in order to occupy my mind and make this boring section a little more interesting, I decided to start counting the moose poop piles as I hiked along.

I hadn't even made it past ten when I noticed something off to my right in the woods. It was a huge moose in the woods. I was really excited because I had never seen a moose in the woods before. It wasn't quite as large as other moose I had seen along the roadside, and it didn't have a rack. It appeared to be a juvenile as opposed to an adult. It was just hanging out, chewing on the leaves of a tree. I'm sure Vaida saw it, but as soon as I stopped to look at it, she did her normal thing and laid down. The moose didn't scare her, and apparently, she didn't scare the moose. It just continued to eat.

I was there for at least five minutes taking pictures, totally in awe of this big beast casually munching away on the leaves of the tree. Vaida treated this stop like any old break, lying down and relaxing the entire time. She probably looked over her shoulder at the moose every now and then but didn't really seem to care that this massive animal was standing about fifteen feet right behind her. I would think most dogs would either bark at it or run away, but not Vaida. She just took a break.

After the encounter, I thought about the fact that the mother might have been around. But I think that once they become "teenagers," the parents let them be on their own. Maybe it was just old enough that we didn't have to worry about the mom. Maybe I should learn more about moose.

10

Our Final Hikes Together

When I first adopted Vaida and throughout her early years with me, I was aware of the fact that someday I would have to deal with the end of her life. I always knew that eventually there would be a really sad day in my future, but I never really thought about the fact that leading up to that, there would be an actual decline in her physical abilities or her ability to go everywhere with me. I had this skewed and unrealistic vision that she would be my adventure partner and sidekick up until the bitter end.

In the summer of 2018, I resigned myself to the fact that I could only take Vaida on hikes in cooler temperatures.

In May of 2018, Jodeob, who was originally from Missouri, wanted to head home to visit family and friends. Vaida and I, of course, went along, and I, of course, asked if we could hike while we were down there. Jodeob obliged, saying we could hike the Buffalo River Trail, a forty-mile trail in Northwest Arkansas that he had hiked before and knew well. To me, forty miles was nothing for Vaida. It would take us two to three days max.

When Jodeob and I decided to take the trip to Missouri, we planned to spend as much time as possible camping. We had all the necessary gear, there were tons of places to camp, and campsites were way cheaper than motels or hotels. What we hadn't planned on was the hot and humid southern weather. And even though we weren't being overly active, spending the majority of our time hanging out at our campsite, there was no getting away from the humidity and high temperatures. All three of us were really hot the entire time.

We were looking forward to the hike on the Buffalo River Trail because the weather was calling for slightly cooler temperatures in Arkansas. Because Jodeob had hiked it before, I relied on his knowledge of the trail to be sure we were well prepared. I constantly asked him before leaving if there would be enough water for Vaida to drink and to cool off in. That seemed like a silly question, given that it was called the Buffalo River Trail, but I just wanted to be sure. If the weather became hot, humid, and sunny, Vaida would need to be able to cool down whenever she wanted. Jodeob assured me that because it followed a river, there would be plenty of places for her to get in and take a swim.

When we first started hiking, even though the trail paralleled the river, I was disappointed to see that there was a steep drop-off between the trail and the river's edge. Vaida wouldn't be able to get down to the water and back up the steep slope, so she never did. We spent the whole day hiking, covering sixteen miles that first day, stopping at a campground that had river access. Vaida didn't seem very tired or lethargic while we were hiking, but by the time we stopped and set up our tent, she was so worn out that she didn't even want to go in the river.

Vaida was clearly exhausted and affected by the heat from that day. She was panting and breathing heavily and wouldn't move. We weren't able to get her to eat, and she barely even drank water from her camp bowl. She literally wouldn't move. It was scary. I'd never seen anything like that happen to her when she was hiking, and it worried me.

Here we were, sixteen miles away from our truck at this campground with a hundred-pound dog that didn't want to move. I continued to try to get her to drink water, but she showed no interest in anything other than lying down and panting heavily. The next morning, we decided we needed to abort the hike and get Vaida out of the heat. I stayed at the campsite with Vaida while Jodeob managed to hitchhike out of the campground. When he returned with the truck, he told me this exciting story about finding a bike with a flat tire on the side of the road and using it to go flying down a big hill, back to the truck. I was just thankful his bike adventure had made his return faster so that we could focus on

Vaida. She and I had been waiting at the campsite for a few hours, and she wasn't showing any signs of getting better.

She was still panting heavily and completely uninterested in moving at all. After a lot of encouragement, we were able to get her in the truck and headed back to Missouri where we had been camping. We knew we couldn't spend another day or night outside in the heat and decided to rent a hotel room so that we could get Vaida into some air conditioning. The fact that Vaida wasn't doing well on the Arkansas hike came as a complete surprise to me after we'd just spent the spring doing what we normally did, hiking in New England. But a spring hike in New England is significantly different from one in the southern United States. Generally, it's going to be pretty comfortable and cool even if you're a hundred-pound dog with a thick Lab/Newfie coat. But hiking in the South was totally different.

With the air conditioning cranked, she just lay around, soaking it in, but still didn't want to eat or move around much. In an effort to get her to eat, I even went to the store and bought her a bunch of canned dog food, thinking surely she'd eat that treat. I mixed the canned wet food in with her crunchies, and this seemed to help, but I was still concerned, so I called my vet back in Vermont. He confirmed that she was likely heat exhausted and to keep an eye on her. As long as she was eating and drinking, even if it was only a little, she should be fine. He probably also told me not to take her hiking when it was ninety degrees out with 100 percent humidity. Finally, after four or five days in the air conditioning, she slowly returned back to her normal self.

Vaida's recovery from this failed hike was way longer than I anticipated. She didn't really move much or want to go anywhere or do anything for almost a week. It wasn't that she was sick—she didn't get sick until the fall of 2021. She was just old and worn out. At the time, she was nine years old and weighed between ninety and a hundred pounds. Over those nine years, she'd logged countless miles and hiked countless peaks, far too many for me to even calculate. When we were on overnight camping trips, we often hiked from sunup to sundown, set up camp, ate, slept, then got up the next day at sunrise and did it all over again. However, it was becoming increasingly clear that hiking the big miles at this stage of her life had taken a toll on her and would continue to take a toll on her. It was slowly becoming apparent that she was no longer capable of a "regular" hiking day.

That May 2018 aborted Arkansas hike was the first clue that she wasn't able to keep up with her old way of life. When it was colder out, she seemed to handle it much better, because she had full hiking seasons in the fall of 2017 and winter of 2018. Jodeob suggested no more hot weather hiking for Vaida, though I already knew her body couldn't handle it anymore. Vaida was my dog, but Jodeob cared for and about her as if she were his too. I trusted his instincts and respected his opinion and knew that he was right. Once we returned to New England, Vaida still hiked, but we paid close attention to the weather forecast and were very selective about the hikes we chose.

In June 2018, a friend of Jodeob's from Georgia, Gas Tank, was visiting family in Vermont. He reached out and told us how he was planning to hike up Mount Mansfield with his son, Ben. Jodeob had met Gas Tank in 2016 when they were both hiking the Appalachian Trail. I have no idea why he was called Gas Tank. It was his trail name. Sometimes you just go with it, without asking questions.

Mount Mansfield is the highest peak in Vermont and a mountain that holds some very special memories from my early hiking days, both as I matured as a hiker and also with a young Vaida. Jodeob and I decided to join Gas Tank and Ben on the hike. Of course, I wanted to bring Vaida. It was only supposed to be in the seventies that day, so I convinced Jodeob to let Vaida try one more hike before laying low for the rest of the summer. Not knowing how well Vaida would fare, we planned a reasonable hike that included taking the shortest, easiest route to the summit of the 4,395-foot mountain. Vaida didn't have any issues while hiking that day. She probably lucked out because Ben was pretty tired by the time we reached the top and, as a group, we decided to take the ski trails down the mountain. This was an easier route than what we had hiked up. Turns out that five-mile hike in June 2018 was the last time Vaida went on a summer hike. Mount Mansfield was one of the first mountains Vaida had climbed as a young pup, so I guess that was a good one to end her summer hiking adventures with.

In order to still get our outdoor fix, we spent the rest of the summer camping rather than hiking. Instead of summiting mountains, we'd find a campground that was on a lake or a river and take Vaida there. We could park next to the tent and take her on short woods walks or strolls around the water, just not all-day ten- or fifteen-mile hikes. Vaida loved swimming and chasing after sticks and balls, and I looked at it as a good way for her to still get exercise while doing something she enjoyed. I could see the same glimmer in her eye and smile on her face when she grabbed the stick that I saw when she was out on the trail. I saw the same tail wag when she tossed the stick on the ground and rolled on top of it that I saw when she met a fellow hiker on the top of a mountain. I did miss hiking with her though, so when the fall and cool temperatures rolled around, I considered taking her on hikes again and Jodeob thought she would be fine, so we did.

Vaida and I went on one of her last New Hampshire hikes that fall. I will never forget that overnight trip in the Presidential Range, hiking from Crawford Notch to Gray Knob. Gray Knob was our favorite cabin in the White Mountains, run by the Randolph Mountain Club, and is the perfect place to stay when you're spending time in the Presidential Range. The Presidential Range contains the highest peaks in the White Mountains, including Mount Washington and seven other four-thousand-plus-foot mountains and the largest expanse of above-tree-line hiking in the state. Despite *only* being 6,288 feet tall, Mount Washington is known for having some of the worst weather on Earth, mainly because of the unpredictability of the weather regardless of the season. It sounds crazy that one mountain in New Hampshire would have this reputation, but it's true. It once held the record for the highest wind speed ever recorded on Earth at 231 miles per hour. In January of 2018, the Mount Washington Observatory recorded a temperature of -36 degrees Fahrenheit, tying it for the second coldest place on the planet, and in February of 2023, the wind chill reached -109 degrees, making it the coldest wind chill ever recorded in the United States. Vaida and I had spent a lot of time in this area, always paying close attention to the forecasts coming from the Mount Washington Weather Observatory.

This particular weekend, the weather forecast looked nearly perfect, so Vaida and I planned to do a twenty-mile Presidential Traverse over two days. We would spend the night at Gray Knob, a small cabin about a mile and a half from the summit of Mount Adams and finish the traverse the next day. That first day was a beautiful fall day. With a mix of clouds and sun, fifty-degree temperatures, and the crisp fall air, the weather couldn't have been more perfect. We made it up to Mount Pierce and were going to be above-tree-line with beautiful views all the way over to Gray Knob, so we chose to bypass the summits of Mount Eisenhower and Mount Monroe and head straight over to Mount Washington. We had hiked approximately seven miles at this point, and I was optimistic that Vaida still had some big mountain hiking in her. We summited Mount Washington and had about five miles left to hike in order to make it to Gray Knob. The hike up to Mount Washington was no problem, but while hiking the section between Mount Washington and Gray Knob, Vaida was having trouble. Her panting became heavier, and she kept stopping and lying down. We had just taken a break and the air was cool, but she just didn't want to hike anymore.

It hurt me seeing her like this, but we had no choice. We had to get to Gray Knob, the place where we were staying, the only safe place to stay. I had my tent with me, but camping is not allowed on this section of trail above-tree-line. We had nowhere else to go. As we continued on the trail, Vaida was stopping and lying down more often and it was starting to get late, so I had to keep encouraging her and we finally made it to Gray Knob. The next day, rather than finish up the traverse, which would mean skipping Mount Adams and Mount Madison, I decided to take a three-mile trail that led from the cabin directly back down to the valley to make it easier for Vaida. I may have pushed Vaida too hard, expecting her to hike twelve miles in really rugged terrain that first day, but it was an indication that she truly was starting to slow down. It wasn't a weather or temperature-related thing. She was getting older, and she was worn out from the years of hiking. I will always remember this attempted full Presidential Traverse I wound up calling "The Vaidadential Traverse."

It had become very clear that no matter the time of year, these overnight backpacking trips were too much for her. There was too much risk when we had to rely on finding a safe place to camp and making sure that we got to it. She was starting to show signs that she couldn't do it, even when we didn't have to worry about her overheating or needing water. It seemed like shorter day hikes were still an option, though, and a few weeks later, she had no problem hiking Mount Moosilauke.

In January of 2019, I took Vaida for a day hike on Franconia Ridge with some friends and their dog who was the same age as Vaida. Though Vaida was starting to slow down, I was confident that a cold winter day would be the best day for her to still get some hiking in. I also thought that having hiked this nine-mile loop at least twenty times together, it would feel very familiar and routine. It would be like we weren't even hiking, just doing what we always did. And routine it was. We hiked the three-and-a-half miles up to the tree line, and Vaida took a break like she always did. Then we hiked 0.7 miles across the ridge to Mount Lincoln for another break. It was another mile to Mount Lafayette, where Vaida always liked to take her longest break, and then three-and-a-half miles back down in a big circle. Vaida proved she could still handle a day hike in the cold winter weather.

Unfortunately, just a few months later, in April, Jodeob, Vaida, and I hiked that same loop for the last time. We hiked it in reverse, making it all the way up Mount Lafayette, across to Mount Lincoln, and the remainder of the ridge with no problem. Vaida ambled along like she always did and seemed to be taking her normal breaks and taking in the very familiar landscape. It was when we began our hike down that Vaida started fading, like she had done on our "Vaidadential Traverse" the previous fall. She kept lying down, taking long breaks, and struggling to get up.

Even though there was still a bunch of snow around, that particular spring day was sunny and warm. Vaida would walk for a minute or two and then lie back down. We realized trying to get down the mountain this way wasn't working. We couldn't keep making her get up and walk for a minute or two before laying back down. Because we were on a steep section of trail that still had snow and ice on it, Jodeob decided that he would sit down and do what was called a "butt slide." He would bear hug her and slide down the mountain with Vaida in his lap.

The trail we were on was called Falling Waters Trail, named after the three waterfalls the trail follows. It was scary because the terrain was really steep and followed a path adjacent to rushing mountain waters. The worst part was that it didn't go straight. It had several hard turns. If he was butt sliding down the mountain, holding Vaida, and not able to stop himself before the turn, they would both go flying into the water.

I remember watching Jodeob do three or four butt slides and stopping himself before the trail turned. I knew it was dangerous for him and for her, and while it was scary to watch, I was confident he would ensure both of their safety. He had a hundred-pound dog in his lap. Through skill, determination, and a little bit of luck, I'm sure, he was able to get her down the steepest part of the trail. The trail eventually flattened out two miles from the parking lot and, while the stress of them sliding into the water eased, the stress of making it back to the car did not. There were really no more steep declines, so Jodeob couldn't butt slide anymore. We had to try and have her walk with us. The same thing happened again. She'd walk a few minutes and lie down. I said, "Jodeob, this isn't working. We're not going to make it back to the car like this. We've got to get some help."

I started thinking about all of the people I could call who lived or hiked in the area, and we were able to get hold of our friend from The Notch Hostel, Justin. He was thirty minutes away and said he'd get there as quickly as he could. While we waited for him, we covered a little more ground by encouraging Vaida to keep moving.

Justin hiked over a mile as fast as he could to meet up with us. He and Jodeob decided that the best option would be for them to take turns carrying Vaida. In order to avoid having to put her down and pick her up again each time they switched, they figured it was best to pass her back and forth every few minutes. I imagine it was not easy carrying a hundred-pound dog down a mountain trail. Vaida, with her tail wagging, seemed to be enjoying the free ride.

Just as they were setting her down in the parking lot, we ran into a woman and her husband who were pulling out. The woman asked, "Is everything okay? We met you guys up on the ridge with your dog."

As luck would have it, her husband was a veterinarian, so he immediately got out of the car and took a look at Vaida. He listened to her heart with his ear and looked at her gums and told me that she was probably a little dehydrated and might have some slight heat exhaustion. I realized that Vaida had been eating snow on the way up and when we were on the ridge, but we hadn't let her go near the water on the way down because it was moving too fast. He went on to tell me that if we brought her home, gave her fluids, food, and rest, she should be fine in a couple of days.

It was very reminiscent of the Arkansas trip. For a few days, she didn't want to move around much. She just wanted to rest.

In June 2019, I wanted to take Vaida up Mount Moosilauke one last time. We had hiked Moosilauke at least forty times together, in every month of the year, and it had always been my favorite mountain to hike with her. I was leaving for the Appalachian Trail in a couple of weeks and would be gone for five months. I knew in my heart that this would be my last chance to ever hike that mountain with Vaida. After the April hike on Franconia Ridge, I was a little leery about whether or not she would be able to do it, but it was an easier hike and it had become so routine over the years that maybe she could. We were going on the hike with my friend from Ibex, Amanda, and her dog, Rye. Rye was young and spry and liked to scamper ahead and chase chipmunks. Vaida was doing her typical ambling along, but two miles into the hike, three-quarters of the way up, she did exactly what she had done on Franconia Ridge. She kept stopping and lying down.

I knew right away that there was no way Vaida was going to make it to the top of the mountain and I had to get her back down. I told Amanda that she and her dog should keep going. They didn't have to turn around with Vaida and me. We could just meet them at the car.

She said, "Are you sure?"

I said, "Yes, of course, you guys go ahead and summit. Vaida will be fine. We just need to turn around and head down."

Vaida needed to take a lot of breaks for water and rest, and it required a lot of encouragement to get her back up, but I was able to slowly hike her down the mountain.

I had really wanted to hike Moosilauke with Vaida one more time. We'd had the situation in Arkansas the previous summer, then the situation on Franconia Ridge in April that we'd thought was also heat exhaustion. Maybe she had improved enough health-wise that Moosilauke was doable on a cool June day. She had shown signs that she was back to normal, at least when she wasn't hiking. She still loved chasing after sticks and playing with her Jolly Ball. She appeared healthy enough that she could still be a trail dog, but this hike proved I was being overly optimistic. Vaida's physical abilities, at least as far as hiking was concerned, were waning.

I left for the Appalachian Trail later that month, and Vaida, who was now ten, went to my parents' house until I returned in November. She essentially spent those five months in retirement. For those rare occasions when I did take trips and did have to leave Vaida behind—whether it was when I was on tour with Grace Potter, a week-long hiking vacation on the West Coast, or a tropical beach vacation—my parents were always glad to take care of her. I never had to take her to a kennel because they were always willing to take her. Caring for Vaida for five months was no problem. They had their dog, Jill, a twelve-year-old golden retriever, so I figured the old ladies could hang out together. Even though Vaida's hiking days were probably over, I still wanted her to get some exercise and move around. My parents said they would take her on walks and take her swimming as much as possible. I believed taking her swimming was the best thing for her and her joints.

My mom probably didn't want a big, wet, hundred-pound dog in her house every day, so Vaida didn't get to go swimming as much as I had hoped. When she did go for a walk, it was a short one around the block. I knew that wasn't Vaida's style and that she preferred hiking in the woods, but she just couldn't do it anymore. I guess by this time she was just more content sleeping on the couch with Jill than she would have been strolling around the block. My parents said that often it took a lot of encouragement to even get Vaida to go outside to do her business. Apparently, getting up from the couch was not on Vaida's retirement agenda.

On June 15, 2019, I started my Appalachian Trail southbound hike in Maine, alone, without my constant hiking companion, and by August I had made it to Connecticut. I had spent the past two months and seven hundred miles feeling like I was walking toward Vaida through familiar territory and sections of New England we had experienced together on previous hikes, familiar trails, mountain peaks, and hundreds of miles that we had hiked together over the years. It was time to see Vaida. I called my parents and asked them to come meet me. I really wanted to experience hiking with Vaida on this tremendous journey of mine, even if only for a short time. My parents met me in Connecticut, where we spent the night in a hotel. I was happy to be able to relax and spend some extra time with Vaida. The next morning, we drove to the trailhead where my parents had picked me up the previous day, and all four of us started hiking south together. Vaida, ambling way slower but taking the lead as usual, managed about a quarter mile before deciding she was done hiking. She stopped and lay down to rest. She was almost eleven and only hiked a quarter mile with me, but it filled my heart with joy to watch her amble along as I recalled my thoughts from the previous seven hundred miles. I had often found myself thinking, *How on earth did Vaida make it up this rocky scramble?!* or *I can't believe Vaida pushed consecutive twenty-five-mile days over this terrain!*

Vaida had logged a lot of miles on the Appalachian Trail with me over the years. This was a section we had never been on together before. Even though it was only a quarter mile, it was special. This was our last hike on the A.T. together.

11

Our Final Days Together

After the Arkansas incident, it was a very hard decision to begin leaving Vaida at home when I hiked, but taking her with me was no longer an option. She had always gone everywhere with me. That was the expectation. Making that decision to leave her behind didn't feel right, but it was something I had to do.

My passion for hiking had increased ten-fold over the past ten years. By the time she could no longer hike with me, I was so obsessed with hiking that, as much as I loved her and wanted to spend every waking minute with her, I had to have my outdoors and exercise and fresh-air time too. Some days she would relax at home with Jodeob, and other days, he would take her swimming. On occasion, she would be left alone watching the Food Network or listening to classical music. It was always a really terrible feeling packing my backpack, knowing she was watching me get my stuff ready. But somehow, I knew she knew she wasn't capable of hiking, so maybe it wasn't as hard on her as I thought.

I really hated leaving Vaida behind at the house whenever I left for a hike, but even more than that, I truly hated not having her with me while I was hiking. It didn't feel right. I felt like I was always looking for her. Driving to the trailhead, every time I stepped on the brakes in the car, I would look back to see if she had perked up to see where we were going. When we were hiking, I liked to feed her the last bite of whatever I was snacking on. I would be finishing something and turn to give it to her, but she was not with me. It was a really strange feeling. Where was my best friend? I don't know if I had really wrapped my head around it at the time, but looking back, I can say maybe Vaida knew I was doing what I loved, I needed to hike, and was happy that I was still doing it but sad that she wouldn't be joining me. I knew she would be okay with that.

By October 2021, I had moved to southern New Hampshire. Vaida was nearing thirteen at this point, and while she showed no apparent signs of health problems, aside from arthritis, she was definitely showing signs of her old age. She was the same slower version of her slow self. Her behavior, however, had begun to change. I used to have no problem leaving her home alone, but shortly after I moved, I started to notice she was no longer okay with being alone. If I left the apartment to run an errand, she would yelp and bark, something she had never done before. I also started to notice that she didn't even like being in a different room, but it was as if she was too tired to get up and follow me. If I wasn't sitting on the floor next to her, petting her, I ran the risk of her yelping for my attention. This behavior was really strange, but I just chalked it up to her adjusting to yet another move and change in scenery.

Shortly after this move, I took her to a vet near where I was living for her annual visit and routine checkup. Throughout Vaida's whole life I had taken her to the same vet in Hinesburg, Vermont, to Dr. Rich Armstrong. Even when I moved an hour and a half away to central Vermont, he was still her primary veterinarian. When I first moved to New Hampshire in 2019, I tried to continue to see him when I could, but it didn't always make sense to drive all that way for routine visits or flea and tick medicine, so I made sure to always have a vet in my local area. Because Vaida also spent time with my mom in Massachusetts, she would also see my mom's vet. No matter which vet we did see, after each visit I would have her records sent to Dr. Armstrong.

Vaida was surprisingly healthy for a dog her age. About the only thing "wrong" with her at this point was arthritis in her hind legs and a couple of noncancerous lumps, a common condition in older dogs. She didn't seem bothered by them. The one near her front leg, however, did cause her to walk with a hitch in her step. Basically, she limped. The vet assured me that I shouldn't worry about them, so I didn't. Routine blood work was also done during this local New Hampshire vet visit, and although a couple of the results were elevated, the vet didn't find it alarming. The only thing she told me was that her white blood cell count was high, but that it was no big deal. All was well, for now.

A couple of weeks later, I ended up on a random, last-minute hiking trip out to the West Coast. I would be spending three days in Zion National Park and then visiting my brother in San Diego, California. While visiting, I planned to hike the first fifty miles of the Pacific Crest Trail and then I would fly back home to Vaida. Vaida went to stay with my parents. A few days after she got there, Vaida was enjoying a very brief play session, rolling around on the grass with her Jolly Ball, when my mom noticed that one of her small lumps had opened up and was slowly bleeding. My mom didn't want to bother me while I was hiking, so she did her "mom" thing and made an appointment for Vaida with her vet. While at the vet, she asked about the large lump near Vaida's leg, thinking it might be making it harder for Vaida to walk. The vet said the lump was a lipoma, a fatty tumor and not cancerous. It could be removed, but that would require putting Vaida under anesthesia. Putting a dog under anesthesia always carried risks but more so as the dog aged. Additionally, in preparation for the surgery, Vaida would have to have some bloodwork and an ultrasound. My mom knew that having the surgery wasn't her decision to make and she would have to talk to me, but scheduled the bloodwork and the ultrasound in case I did want to have the lipoma removed.

When the bloodwork came back, the results were the same as what the New Hampshire vet's had read. Vaida's white blood cell count was elevated and, according to my mom's vet, something wasn't right. Something was off. The ultrasound was done a few days after I returned from my trip and provided the reason for the elevated levels. Vaida had a large soccer-ball-sized mass in her abdomen.

The vet told me that they'd have to do a lot more tests to find out if it was cancer, and that would be expensive. If it was cancer, Vaida would have to undergo a massive surgery that was very risky at her age. The vet could not assure me she would survive the surgery, or that it would give us much more time together. On the other hand, the mass could rupture if it was not removed. Toward the end of the conversation, she said, "Some people in this situation do consider putting their dog down. That's something to think about." I was completely taken aback, not prepared to hear this at all. Over the years, I had heard plenty of stories of friends being in similar situations with their dogs, but not my girl Vaida. It couldn't be.

I didn't even need to think about it and simply said, "She's eating, she's drinking, she's going to the bathroom. She's fine. She does not need to be put down."

I was completely blown away that the vet would even ask me to consider putting my dog down. In fact, I was really upset. This was completely out of left field. I now knew that there was something going on with Vaida aside from old age and arthritis, but it was by no means the time for either one of us to call it quits. For almost thirteen years, Vaida had been my other half. She was a piece of me, and the thought of her no longer being with me was simply incomprehensible.

I took her back to New Hampshire with me. The first few days back at home, she seemed like the old, normal but slower version of Vaida, but she was also exhibiting this new Vaida. The Vaida that would bark and yelp when I left the room. The Vaida that didn't want to let me out of her sight. Things really started to change the night she woke me up because she needed to go outside. It was the middle of the night, and this was unusual. Once outside, she basically fell over and was having a hard time getting back up. When she was finally able to get back up, she was wobbling and couldn't walk a straight line. My heart sank, but once again I convinced myself of a reason why it had happened. Maybe she had eaten something she shouldn't have?

I honestly don't know why that happened, but all signs were pointing to things starting to decline pretty rapidly with her. I just kept clinging to the fact that she was still eating and drinking. It just didn't seem like she should be done with life.

I spent the next two weeks with Vaida, in my room, as her body was slowly giving out. Because of the recent move, I was between jobs and wasn't working at the time. I had planned to start working again soon, but it became glaringly obvious that I couldn't leave her alone at home. She was really needing me and wanting to be with me, around me, next to me, and I wanted to be with her too.

Over the next couple of weeks, we spent all of our time together in my bedroom, just being together. I lived simply. We shared my bed, which was a mattress on pallets on the floor. She would tell me when she needed to go out to do her business. She was eating her crunchies like normal each morning and night. She was still drinking and had an appetite, but really all she wanted to do was lie next to me and sleep. I spent two straight weeks with us being together, making sure she was fed, doing her business, and loving her. I was so overwhelmed by the thought that Vaida might be nearing the end of her life that I can't recall any of the specifics or details of that timeframe. It is a complete blur. All I know is that I was worried, sad, and distraught and did everything that I possibly could to show her how much I loved her.

I finally allowed myself to come to the realization that things weren't right. Vaida was starting to suffer, and I was suffering watching her suffer. I called my mom and said, "Something's really wrong with Vaida. She's really not doing well." I still wasn't ready to put her down, but I also knew that when it was time, the vet that I wanted to do it was Dr. Armstrong. I also really wanted him to be able to see her one last time, but he was three hours away. Sure, I could have driven Vaida the three hours to northern Vermont, but then I would have had a long, lonely, sad three-hour drive back alone. I couldn't do that. When I told my mom what was going on, she said I should come home. She and my dad wanted to be there for me, and the vet who had seen Vaida most recently was there too.

When I got to my parents' house, I thought Vaida still had time and I'd get to spend another week or two or three with her. She may have been a little uncomfortable, but I had myself convinced she wasn't in actual pain. Whatever was going on, being with family would make things easier. I got to my parents' house in the afternoon, and as soon as I got there, my mom could see that Vaida was *very* uncomfortable. She said, "Caitlin, I agree, she is not doing well. You know what you have to do. You don't want her to suffer." I knew she was right, and even though I didn't feel ready, I was pretty sure Vaida was. We made an appointment for the following morning.

I spent that entire night up and awake with Vaida, my last twenty-four hours with her. I wanted to soak up as much time with her as I could, and I think Vaida wanted to do the same. It was as if she knew this was our last night together.

As the night wore on, it became abundantly clear to me that Vaida was now physically uncomfortable. Every five or ten minutes, she moved around and changed positions, going from next to me on my mattress, which I had set up on the floor, to the floor and back again, making quiet noises while trying to put her body into a more comfortable position. She would fall asleep briefly, for just a few minutes, then try to get up and move. Maybe she was thirsty or wanted to eat something. She wasn't really able to get to the water bowl or the food bowl, so I brought it to her.

That entire night was terrible. Vaida was incapable of moving herself around, and I had to help her get her hind quarters up by lifting the dog mat under her. I gave her food throughout the night and fed her treats constantly. I couldn't believe her time was almost over. How was this possible? She was still eating. I kept thinking she couldn't possibly be ready to go if she was still desiring food and water.

I was also convinced that Vaida was suffering emotionally from the realization that her time was near and that she would soon be leaving the person with whom she had spent her entire life. It was almost as if she could read my mind, knowing how much I dreaded losing her and wanting to capture every last waking moment that we could.

Before I knew it, it was morning and we had to leave for the vet's office soon. There was this very odd, quiet feeling in the air. I imagined my parents were worried about me and wanted to give me space as I processed everything. The hardest part of that morning at the house was when it was time to leave and we had to get Vaida in the car. Her ability to get up and move around had drastically diminished seemingly over-night. She was a big, big dog, and her once-strong rear legs, which had propelled her up so many mountain peaks, could no longer support her. She couldn't get up, especially in a place that had hardwood floors. It was painful for her, and it was painful for me to watch.

After about twenty minutes, we settled her into the back seat of the car and were about to leave when my mom said, "Oh, wait a second." She ran back into the house and brought out a bag of steak tips. "For Vaida," she said.

I was really glad that my mom thought of that, but I couldn't believe I hadn't thought of some really nice final treat for her. Vaida was my best friend. I'd spent almost thirteen years with her and should have been the one to come up with this great idea, some last way to give her something special. I realize now that I was in a state of complete shock. Consumed by grief and sadness, I couldn't believe these were Vaida's final hours with me. I couldn't believe we had just put Vaida in the car and were taking her to the vet to say goodbye.

My memory of our time at the vet's office is one of my least favorite memories, but is just as much an important part of this story as the peaks Vaida climbed and the miles she hiked. When you go to the vet's office, the staff is really sensitive and caring. They tell you to spend as much time as you want before the vet comes in to dispense the medication. I didn't spend very much time there, because I spent the entire night with her and did most of my talking to her and saying goodbye in the morning at my parents' house. I was in a weird, sterile vet office. I didn't need to do much more.

Fortunately, they "prepped" Vaida in a back exam room, so I didn't have to watch that part of the process. I made sure to hug and hold her when they finally came back in to administer. I couldn't look at the vet or what her hands were doing with Vaida. Honestly, it didn't take long before the vet said, "She's passed."

The vet left the office to give me some time to grieve. I was sobbing and wailing and shaking uncontrollably. I had never felt such raw pain and sadness in my life. When we left the office, I asked my mom, "On a scale of one to ten, how bad was I in there?" She responded with, "Caitlin, I'm pretty sure the entire vet's office could hear you," and proceeded to give me a big comforting mom hug. I was still sobbing and shaking.

The hardest part had been looking at her lying motionless on the floor. Maybe you're supposed to do that, but seeing her on the floor not moving or breathing was heart wrenching. That vivid memory was burned into my head for weeks after, and I kept wishing I hadn't looked.

Although I think about Vaida often, I haven't thought about that day in quite a while, and I am much more in control of my emotions now. When I do look back on that day, of course, it makes me really sad. But when I look back on my relationship with her and our time together, it helps to make me a little less sad. There were so many incredible experiences that we had and so many amazing things that we did together. There are so many lives she touched and memories she made that I would rather tell people about how amazing my dog was and about the great life we shared. I'm not going to sit here and be sad and let sadness be the greatest feeling.

The best example I can give about not dwelling on the negative was a funny moment the day I put Vaida down. Once all of the preparations were made, Vaida was brought into the room where my parents and I were waiting. I brought Vaida's Mutt Mat, her favorite blanket, for her to lie on, and I lay next to her. The vet tech said to me, "Spend as much time with her as you want. When you're ready, walk over to this keypad on the wall and push button number five underneath the blue button. That tells us that you're ready for us to come in."

There we all were, Vaida, my parents, and me, in this bland, sterile room without the familiar comforts of home, just a hard floor, a cabinet full of vet supplies, and a wooden bench. Vaida lay on her Mutt Mat, I lay on the floor next to her, my parents sat on the bench. After just a few minutes, I turned to my parents and said, "I already said goodbye to her and talked to her and spent all night and morning with her. I've never done anything like this before. I guess I'm ready." I hated being here like this. My mom said she and dad had already said their goodbyes too, so I walked over to the wall, pressed the button, then sat back down next to Vaida and fed her more steak tips.

There was also a jar of treats on the counter. I kept walking over, taking treats, and giving them to Vaida. After five minutes had gone by, I was wondering where the vet was. Ten minutes went by, fifteen minutes went by, still no one. It was agonizing and had even started to get annoying. I pressed the button just like I was told to, but no one came. I spent all morning saying goodbye to her, so these fifteen minutes waiting felt like an eternity. After twenty minutes, I was pretty upset. I think my mom was getting upset too, seeing how mad I was, especially because I was mad at *her* vet.

Even though this was probably one of the worst moments of my life, I was able to add an array of humor to this absolutely devastating event. To hide the deep sense of heartbreak and pain I was feeling, I was making jokes, saying "This is fucking ridiculous. This is torture. They better be giving me a discount!" All three of us were able to share a laugh during this incredibly sad moment.

Finally, after an excruciatingly long twenty minutes, my mom looked at me and said, "What button did you press?"

I said, "I pressed the blue button."

She said, "Caitlin, they said press button number five *underneath* the blue button!"

I got up and pressed button five. Sure enough, the vet came in thirty seconds later.

There's always been a lot of laughter and humor shared among me and my family and friends. It's nice to have a lighthearted moment come out of an otherwise very sad moment, and to be able to tell a funny story about it. It was my fault, after all. I'd pressed the wrong button. There's been a few times since that day that I've heard the words "blue button" and it doesn't make me sad; it always seems to make me laugh. I think Vaida would have liked this story too.

I had always said when Vaida passed I was going to get on a long-distance trail to walk off my grief. My intention was for this to be a four- to five-month-long hike, but it was November, not a typical start time for any of the major trails. Plus, I had to start working again. Friends of mine who I had met on the Appalachian Trail in Maine earlier that summer happened to be on a section of the trail not too far from my folks' house. This was perfect! Now I could still say that when Vaida passed, I went and got on a long-distance trail.

My dad offered to drive me to Connecticut to meet up with Disco, Snocket, and Goat so that we could hike south on the A.T. together for a week. During the car ride, my dad and I were chatting. He could tell that I was still very sad and really missed Vaida. This was the first time I had been at my parents' house in twelve years without her. I couldn't even sleep in the same room where Vaida and I had spent our last twenty-four hours together. It was too much of a painful reminder that she was no longer here. Everywhere I looked, something reminded me of her. Sensing my pain, my dad said to me, "Just remember those last twenty-four hours. Remember what you went through with her that night. You did the right thing. Remember the amount of suffering that she was going through, and that you went through."

He was right. I had been second guessing my decision a little. In the weeks leading up to that day, she was still eating and drinking. Other than her difficulty getting up and moving around more slowly, both of which I attributed to her old age, she didn't seem to be suffering. But as I reflected back on our last twenty-four hours, staying up all night with her and seeing how uncomfortable she was, it was confirming to me that this was the right decision. I'm sure I was initially holding onto the idea that she could somehow miraculously get better. Looking back at it, there was no way we could have done anything differently. I think that when we spent that last day and night awake together, in those twenty-four hours, she had a terrible time because she had hung on for so long and was determined to stay with me. She didn't want to let go, and she wasn't ready to, but she needed to. That was her final moment of being as close to me as she could be, and then she just couldn't do it anymore. It really was time.

12

Forever and Always

When I'd adopted Vaida, it was simply because I wanted a companion. Someone to always be by my side. Never did I think that she would completely change my life. Vaida helped me gain confidence as a hiker, taught me more about myself than I could have ever learned on my own, changed the way I see the world, and helped me see how I want to live my life. When I reflect back on the person I was compared with the person I am today, I see a more confident and outgoing version of myself, living life minimally and in the moment. I have learned to live life on a day-to-day basis with not much care beyond that of love and compassion for others and those around me. What stories I can tell and what I can learn from the stories told to me. I am not married, have no kids, home, mortgage, or debt. I live simply and seek to journey through life with a smile on my face, a positive reflection on the past, and a curiosity for the future. It was my deep connection with Vaida that led me to so many other incredible connections and people. I was able to experience life in a fulfilling way that I never imagined was possible.

Hiking with Vaida was the highlight of our almost thirteen years together. It was because of all of our time spent adventuring outdoors that I truly began to experience personal growth and continued to become a more knowledgeable and experienced hiker. She helped me make connections with well-known and accomplished hikers, countless White Mountains enthusiasts, and more caring and compassionate individuals in hiking communities than I'll ever be able to recall. Hiking is more than putting on a backpack and hiking up a mountain. The variables left unconsidered can be incredibly dangerous. While I may have previously taken more risks than I should have, it became crucial that I consider all of the variables because I needed to take care of Vaida as well as myself.

Vaida was my "icebreaker." Her mere presence and beauty opened the door to conversation with people I would have never previously spoken to. The connections she helped me make and the knowledge I acquired made me wiser and less reckless.

Achieving your anticipated goal when you're out in nature is not really up to you. In the end, the mountains are going to dictate what your fate will be. You may have the perfect day to hike. Your body and mind may feel ready, saying you're going to go climb some mountains. But it's never really up to you because the weather can change at any given moment and the mountains just say, "Not today." That's what would happen with Vaida and me sometimes. We would be on trips or a planned overnight together and quickly learn we didn't always have a true hand to play. We just knew we were starting in one particular place and hoping to get to another. That didn't always happen. Even though these may have been "failed" trips and we often had to rely on perfect strangers to help us out, they remain some of my most memorable adventures with Vaida and serve to remind me not only about the importance of safety but also reinforce my continuing faith in humanity.

I've learned that life works in mysterious ways and there's all sorts of ways to navigate through it. A lot of people have a master plan in mind for where their life should take them, but I've learned that you never know what's going to happen while you're on that path. I found it would make things more interesting not having a true plan or destination, because ultimately, I feel that it's nice to be able to switch course a little bit so you can go with the flow and not miss things planning couldn't have included. It's nice to occasionally just see what happens or who you will meet along the way. My life has been full of serendipitous moments reminding me that most things happen for a reason and that if I continue to breathe good into this world, good things will come my way.

The stories I've shared about our adventures and the people we have met are only a small glimpse into the adventurous and highly social life that Vaida and I led. I've met people from all walks of life, different places in the world, different ages and backgrounds. Just being open to interacting with people and being curious to learn more about them, their life, and what excites and drives them has influenced and inspired me so much. I have Vaida to thank for this.

When I started on the Long Trail, I was intimidated by Appalachian Trail hikers. Vaida was my "friend magnet." I think about the countless friends I've made because of her, and now I can confidently introduce myself to anyone without the fear I once felt. I also think about all of the people I would have never met were it not for her. As I have been working on this book, I've been able to talk about her and share her story and realize that I'm still making friends because of her. Now, whether I'm telling a story about Vaida or talking about life in general, you can't get me to shut up.

My bond with Vaida helped me have the confidence to forge my own bonds with others. I would see her engage with strangers and that prompted me to be more comfortable doing the same. It just made me want to keep doing things with her because it helped me grow to be a stronger, more sociable person and more confident hiker. I now love creating bonds, making relationships, and meeting people. I no longer hesitate to engage with complete strangers, be it a trail angel, a hiker at my campsite, or even the person in front of me in the grocery store line. I just start talking. I truly think you can touch someone in just a moment with something you say or something you have done. You can inspire them, based on your character and your personality and your outlook. In just a very brief moment, you can become a very unforgettable person to them, and they to you.

My journey through life with Vaida was not just a matter of setting out with a specific goal to get from point A to point B. The journey was about everything in between and all that we experienced. The final destination was just a way to end that day's adventures. What truly mattered was the moments we shared, the people we met, the memories we built. It was the experience of doing something together and the things that would happen along the way. Vaida didn't care where we were going. She was just into "going."

As I write this final chapter, it's been exactly one year since I lost my sweet, beautiful girl. My best friend and adventure partner. The greatest yellow dog there ever was. Not a day goes by that I don't think about the almost thirteen years we spent together. This past year has had some challenges but has also been filled with incredible adventure and reflection. Thousands of miles hiked without Vaida and her legacy and the story of our life together being put on paper. I've left Vaida's ashes on dozens of peaks in the White Mountains of New Hampshire as well as the three in Maine she wasn't allowed to visit. I've marveled in the memories and her accomplishments. I've stood on peaks in New Hampshire and gazed at four-thousand-foot mountains in the distance, knowing Vaida rests in all of those places forever.

They say a dog's only fault is that they don't live long enough. I don't think I could fault Vaida for a single thing. The amount of sheer joy, pride, companionship, adventure, and connection to other folks she provided is immeasurable. Over the course of almost thirteen years, Vaida shaped me to be the outgoing, energetic, adventurous, fun-seeking, and charismatic person I am today. I have said it one thousand times this year since Vaida's passing, and I'll say it a million times more. Vaida brought me far too much happiness and too many experiences, memories, and personal growth to ever let sadness be the greatest feeling I have. I may be leaving Vaida's ashes on mountain tops, but she will always be deep in my heart.

I love you forever and always, my sweet girl.

in loving memory of vaida. the greatest yellow
dog there ever was. 12/06/08 - 11/05/21

By the way, it's pronounced "vay-duh."

You'll have to meet another Jodeob to figure out how that's pronounced.

Article about Ibex winning the Purina Pets at Work Contest:
https://www.outsidebusinessjournal.com/press-releases/
ibex-outdoor-clothing-wins-nestle-purina-pets-at-work-contest/

Purina video featuring Caitlin and Vaida:
https://vimeo.com/142530824/9161a4b1ac

Purina video featuring the pet-friendly culture at Ibex:
https://www.martimvian.com/new-page

NBC Nightly News story about Ibex, "A Doggone Friendly Office Breeds Un-Fur-gettable Perk":
https://www.nbcnews.com/video/a-doggone-friendly-office-breeds-un-fur-gettable-perk-347850819766

Osprey's video about Caitlin and ultralight backpacking:
https://www.youtube.com/watch?app=desktop&v=B-g5gdiSh4Y

Osprey's "Omlette Guy" video:
https://www.youtube.com/watch?v=xq5DATG44R8

GearJunkie article about hiking with dogs:
https://gearjunkie.com/proj/explainer-series/
how-to-hike-with-dog-backpacking-trails

Caitlin's blog about hiking the Long Trail with Vaida:
https://caitlinthemoment.wordpress.com

A YEAR IN THE HIKING LIFE

I wanted to give a glimpse into just how much Vaida and I hiked together, so I figured what better way than to look back at a year of photographs and document every single adventure Vaida and I went on together. Unless otherwise noted, she accompanied me on all of these adventures.

To many, this may just be words on paper—mountains you've never heard of, details that mean nothing, and numbers that make no sense—but to me, these words warm my heart and fill me with unforgettable memories, many of which I can still recount without even looking back at the photographs. I'll never forget that year of adventure with Vaida. It was the year we completed the NH48. It was the year that I became the hiker I am today. Perhaps most importantly, it was the year Vaida and I became known as an unforgettable mountain duo.

(4k indicates it was a 4,000-foot mountain)

JANUARY

Jan 1   Short A.T. hike to meet Tom "The Real Hiking Viking" in Maine with Tick Tock

Jan 2   Mt. Field (24/48) with Tick Tock (4K)

Jan 3   Lonesome Lake with Tick Tock

Jan 9   Whiteface and Passaconaway (25/48 & 26/48) (two 4Ks)

Jan 15   Mt. Pierce (4K)

Jan 16   Backcountry skiing with Tick Tock in local Vermont fields

Jan 17   Backcountry skiing with Evan and Jordi on Skyline Trail in Barnard, VT

Jan 20   Skinned up to the top of Suicide Six ski hill with Ibex coworkers

Jan 23   Hiked on the Appalachian Trail from Hanover, NH to West Hartford, VT – 10 miles with Tick Tock, Matt & Tom "The Real Hiking Viking" during his winter A.T. southbound

Jan 24   Mt. Moosilauke (4K)

Jan 30   Mt. Mansfield, the highest peak in Vermont (4K)

Jan 31   Franconia Ridge (two 4Ks)

FEBRUARY

Feb 1   Section hiked on the A.T. near Woodstock, VT

Feb 2   Attempted the Wildcats with Tick Tock and turned around (too icy and steep)

Feb 14   Mt. Hunger in Vermont with Matt – negative 10 degrees; Mt. Washington was second coldest recorded place on Earth on this day

Feb 21   Mt. Moosilauke (4K) – total whiteout conditions

Feb 27   Mt. Mansfield in Vermont with Matt (4K) – entire traverse –Sunset Ridge to Maple Ridge

Feb 28   Mt. Moosilauke (4K)

MARCH

Mar 5	Middle & North Tripyramid (two 4Ks) with Leah D. (27/48 & 28/48)
Mar 6	Franconia Ridge (two 4Ks)
Mar 12	Mt. Moosilauke (4K) (with Jordana & Stacy)
Mar 13	Mt. Monroe (4K) & Mt. Washington (4K)
Mar 19- 28	Arizona Trail with Jason (160 miles – no Vaida)

APRIL

Apr 9	Mt. Carrigain (4K) with Serena & friend (29/48)
Apr 10	Mt. Pierce & Mt. Eisenhower (two 4Ks) (Mt. Eisenhower 30/48)
Apr 15	Mt. Cube in New Hampshire
Apr 16	Mt. Isolation (31/48)
Apr 17	Zealand Bonds Traverse (Zealand, West Bond, Bond & Bondcliff) (four 4Ks) with Serena (32/48) – girls vs. guys, Justin & friend
Apr 21	Castle Trail to Mt. Jefferson (4K) to Israel Ridge with Justin and Serena (33/48)
Apr 23	East Osceola & Mt. Osceola (two 4Ks) (34/48 & 35/48)
Apr 24	Mt. Hale (36/48), Mt. Tom (37/48), Mt. Field & Mt. Willey (38/48) – able to score a hitch back to our car with a gentleman we had met on Hale in the morning (four 4Ks)
Apr 29	Owls Head (4K) (39/48)
Apr 30	Apr 30 Franconia Ridge (two 4Ks)

MAY

May 1	Welch Dickey with Serena & Justin's aunt – turned around due to weather, rain and slick
May 6	Mt. Moosilauke (4K)
May 7	Mt. Ascutney, VT
May 8	North Pack Monadnock, NH

MAY (CONTINUED)

May 12	Wildcat-Carter Traverse – Wildcat D (40/48), Wildcat A (41/48), Carter Dome 42/48), South Carter (43/48) & Middle Carter (44/48) – the day I impaled my leg and we missed Mt. Moriah due to accident (five 4Ks)
May 20	Mt. Waumbek (45/48) & Mt. Cabot (46/48) (two 4Ks)
May 21	Mt. Moriah (47/48) – got stitches removed that day after hike
May 22	Mt. Madison (4K) (FINISHED 48, woooohooo!)
May 28	Gray Knob & summit of Mt. Adams (4K) for sunset; returned to Gray Knob for overnight
May 29	Mt. Jefferson (4K), then Mt. Clay to Mt. Washington (4K) with intention to return to Gray Knob to overnight there. Met family on summit with 2 cars at bases of Mt. Washington & Gray Knob; hiked down with them so I didn't have to hike back to Gray Knob; left gear at Gray Knob and had staff at Mt. Washington radio over to tell them I wouldn't be back there that night and I would pick up my gear the following weekend.

JUNE

June 2	Mt. Ascutney – with Ibex to do trailwork
June 4	June 4 Mount Adams (4K) for sunset, then camped at Gray Knob cabin and retrieved gear left behind the previous weekend
June 10	June 10 Planned 32-mile Pemi Loop; bailed on Mt. Lafayette because of weather – socked in with not much visibility and trees covered in rime ice (four 4ks)
June 11	Mt. Hale (4K) with Christine
June 12	Cannon Mountain (4K)
June 16	Bald Mountain with Serena
June 17-18	Successfully backpacked Pemi Loop for the first time (nine 4Ks)
June 20	Mt. Cardigan
June 24-25	Zealand Bonds Traverse (Zealand, West Bond, Bond & Bondcliff) as overnight with Evan & his sister (four 4Ks)

June 26   Mt. Monroe (4K) & Mt. Washington (4K)

JULY

July 1-2   Grafton Loop – 38 miles (one Maine 4K)

July 3   Baldface Circle Trail – second longest above-tree line stretch in White Mountains

July 4   Wildcats (two 4Ks) with Christine – this was where we met Courtney

July 8   Camels Hump in Vermont (4K) with Laura (aka Spora)

July 16-17   Gray Knob overnight camping with Serena, Mt. Adams & Mt. Jefferson (two 4Ks) the following day
               Beach Break in Rockport

July 26   Mt. Cardigan – after work at Ibex

July 29   Mt. Moosilauke (4K) (start of direttissima)

July 30   South Kinsman (4K), North Kinsman (4K), & Cannon (4K) – decided to ditch direttissima

July 31   Franconia Ridge Loop (two 4Ks)

AUGUST

Aug 3   Mt. Eisenhower (4K)

               Start of long weekends spent on A.T. with Mr. Sunshine

Aug 5-7   Kinsman Notch to Dorchester Road in Lyme, NH – 33.3 miles (one 4K)

Aug 9   2-mile road walk thru Hanover

Aug 12-14   Pomfret Road, VT, to Kent Pond, VT – 24.2 miles

Aug 18-20   US Forest Service Road 10 to Bennington, VT – 57.8 miles

Aug 24   Gile Mountain, VT

Aug 26-28   Bennington, VT, to Cheshire, MA – 32.9 miles

SEPTEMBER

Sept 3-4	Great Barrington, MA, to Salisbury, CT – 29.4 miles
Sept 10	returned to Vermont with Mr. Sunshine and hiked Mt. Mansfield (4K)
	Aruba Beach Vacation Break
Sept 25	Jennings Peak & Sandwich Dome (White Mountains)

OCTOBER

Oct 1	Explored vast network of trails on northwestern side of Northern Presidentials with two friends
Oct 2	Mt. Hale (4K)
Oct 8-10	Long Trail, VT, from Appalachian Gap to Duxbury Rd – 21 miles
Oct 15-16	Mt. Stanton, Mt. Pickering, Mt. Langdon, Mt. Parker, Mt. Resolution, Stairs Mountain (NH) – with Arlette overnight camp
Oct 16	Mt. Isolation (4K) – with Rich after he hiked up to camp and join in
Oct 23	Mt. Ascutney (with Ibex coworkers)
Oct 30	Mt. Moosilauke (4K)

NOVEMBER

Nov 5	Mt. Moosilauke (4K)
Nov 6	Skookumchuck Trail with plan to summit Lafayette, but turned around after breaking tree line due to bad weather – total whiteout and socked in
Nov 12	North Twin (4K) & South Twin (4K) with Courtney & her dad
Nov 13	Franconia Ridge (two 4Ks)
Nov 19	Mt. Madison (4K) & Mt. Adams (4K) with friend Eric; Serena met us and we camped at Gray Knob
Nov 20	Awoke to bad weather – rain – hiked down
Nov 24	Mt. Skinner, MA
Nov 26	Mt. Moosilauke (4K)
Nov 27	Mt. Chocorua

DECEMBER

Dec 3	Mt. Monroe attempt with Peter (turned back at Lakes of the Clouds hut due to weather)
Dec 4	Mt. Moosilauke (4K)
Dec 10	Mt. Pierce (4K) with Christine, Serena, and other friends
Dec 11	Mt. Cube
Dec 15-21	Hiked last 150 miles of the A.T. with Mr. Sunshine in North Carolina and Georgia (Vaida stayed at my parents, sleeping on the couch)
Dec 26	Mt. Tom, MA
Dec 31	Hiked up to Lonesome Lake

ACKNOWLEDGMENTS

First and foremost I'd like to thank my mother Mary Jane Quinn. She has been my number one support throughout this entire process, often literally by my side, and she has continued to encourage me, push me, and love every ounce of me through all the aches and pains of documenting this story. I'd like to thank my father John Quinn because he is where I get my sense of humor from, but thankfully not his propensity to make unsolicited comments that somehow he only finds humorous. And, of course, without him and my mother, I wouldn't be on this planet. I also owe them both much gratitude for their unconditional love and support of my wild and adventurous life. I'd also like to thank my big brother Chris for showing me that family means everything and for his ability to go on incredibly long (but helpful) rants from his big-brother pedestal. I'd especially like to thank him for always reminding me that I am not only cooler than him but a better athlete than him. I'd also like to thank:

- Leah for inspiring me to get a dog and for always wanting "nibble kisses" from Vaida. The love you showered Vaida with is simply remarkable.

- Kevin for loving me and allowing Vaida to come to work at the loud concert hall. Also, for being available to me whenever I was having a tough time in life. Twenty years later and we are still in touch. I love you, Kevin. All of the "HG family" for being so wonderful and looking out for one another. You guys were my best friends.

- Garett for also inspiring me to get a dog by his incredible bond with Jerry. You two showed me that it was possible to take a dog everywhere.

- Ted, Melissa, and all of my dear friends at Ibex. I'd especially like to thank Michael for inspiring and continuing to push me to hike the 48.

- Serena and Justin for creating my home away from home, The Notch Hostel. For sharing your wealth of knowledge with me about hiking in the Whites. For loving me, taking care of me, and boundlessly loving Vaida. Members of "The Hamily"—Declan, Phil, Kale, Jodeob, Steve, Jeremy, Tim, Tricia, and especially Kelly for creating this beautiful cover. This book wouldn't have been possible if all of these people hadn't taught me the joys of the White Mountains and what it's like to truly be part of a community. I'd also like to thank Marleen for always being available to give rides to hikers. I love you all.

- Additional special thanks goes to Kale for your strength, courage, and determination. Always putting up a fight even when things seem impossibly hard. For your boundless spirit, energy, and infectious smile, and for always being there for me.

- Rich and Arlette for being so inspiring by their accomplishments and always being available when I had a question or trepidations.

- Ben Crawford for helping me with questions about writing a book. Also, his beautiful family, well, for being beautiful.

- Marie, Jeff, and Wess of Groundbird Gear for creating beautiful custom packs that Vaida carried on all of her overnight adventures. Oh, and that amazing trail magic when I was on the Appalachian Trail.

- The staff and especially Dr. Rich Armstrong of Hinesburg Animal Hospital for all of the care and love you shared with Vaida and for always calling her "sweet girl."

- My extended family for all of the love and support of all my adventurous, sometimes crazy endeavors. Including the writing of this book.

- And of course Golden Huggs Rescue for bringing the light of my life into my life.

- Randolph Mountain Club for their vast network of trails and for providing our favorite shelters in the Presidential Range.

- All of the trail crews who maintain the trails that Vaida and I tread thousands of miles over.

- The trail community, trail angels, and all of the folks that provide trail magic.

- Tick Tock for allowing a dorky little Long Trail hiker like me to join your trail family on the Appalachian Trail.

- Debra for guiding me and encouraging me through the end of this process and for the beautiful edit. I'd also like to thank you for not allowing this last part to be in lowercase despite the fact that, as all of my friends and family know, I like to type in lowercase and hand write in all uppercase. I wanted to print the whole book like that, but I didn't really think readers would like that.

- Last, I would like to thank Jodeob for loving and adventuring with Vaida for five years and taking care of her as if she were your own. You taught us so much about life and the joys of living simply. I know that Vaida will always be in your heart too.

- And of course Vaida, "my girl," for the love and joy and adventure you brought me. There are almost no words for it. That's not true. There are about 55,000 words in this book, plus the words from the millions of stories I'll tell about you for the rest of my life.

ABOUT THE AUTHOR

Caitlin Quinn is an adventurer and accomplished hiker who loves to meet people, create memories, and share stories. Together with her beloved canine hiking partner, Vaida, she has hiked thousands of miles throughout New England, completing Vermont's Long Trail, the New Hampshire 48, and the New England 67. She repeatedly hiked New Hampshire's peaks as well as the New England sections of the Appalachian Trail with Vaida. In 2019, she followed her dream and solo hiked the entire Appalachian Trail. Caitlin's strength is connecting with people through sharing her adventure stories and memories. She grew up in Amherst, Massachusetts, and, as a true testament to the beginnings of her athleticism, attended the University of Vermont on a softball scholarship. It was there that she kindled her passion for hiking and the outdoors. When she's not traveling, she spends as much time as possible in Vermont and the White Mountains. *My Girl Vaida* is Caitlin's first published work. She has no plans for a sequel, but then again, she never planned to become a passionate hiking adventurer either. Stay tuned.

Stop by the author's website to check out a cool Vaida-inspired T-shirt and sign up for the newsletter: mygirlvaida.com

Connect with the author on Instagram: @cmquinn

www.ingramcontent.com/pod-product-compliance
Lightning Source LLC
Chambersburg PA
CBHW031141130726
47988CB00006B/2474